World Heritage Sites of Britain

Editor: Donna Wood
Designer: Patrick Budge
Picture Researcher: Alice Earle
Image retouching and internal repro: Neil Smith and Marion Morris
Cartography provided by the Mapping Services Department
of AA Publishing
Production: Stephanie Allen

Produced by AA Publishing
© Copyright AA Media Limited 2010
Foreword text © Copyright Griff Rhys Jones

Contains Ordnance Survey data. © Crown Copyright and database right 2010

ISBN: 978-0-7495-6651-7 (T) and 978-0-7495-6660-9 (SS)

Published by AA Publishing (a trading name of AA Media Limited, whose registered office is Fanum House, Basing View, Basingstoke RG21 4EA; registered number 06112600).

A04233

Printed in China by C & C Offset Printing Co. Ltd

theAA.com/shop

This book is dedicated to the memory of
Joyce and Charles Stennett,
my mother- and father-in-law,
who loved these places.

Roly Smith

World Heritage Sites of Britain

Roly Smith
Foreword by Griff Rhys Jones

Neolithic Orkney ◈

St Kilda ◈

Antonine Wall ◈ ◈ Edinburgh

New Lanark ◈

Giant's Causeway ◈

Hadrian's Wall ◈

Durham Cathedral & Castle ◈

Studley Royal Park & Fountains Abbey ◈

◈ Saltaire

◈ Liverpool

King Edward's Castles ◈

Pontcysyllte Aqueduct ◈

◈ Derwent Valley Mills

Ironbridge ◈

Blenheim Palace ◈

Blaenavon ◈

Tower of London & Westminster ◈

Royal Botanic Gardens ◈

City of Bath ◈

◈ Avebury

◈ Canterbury Cathedral

◈ Maritime Greenwich

Stonehenge ◈

The Jurassic Coast ◈

Cornwall & West Devon Mines ◈

Contents

Foreword

The official, unassailable, list of World Heritage Sites is decided by Unesco. You can apply to have your own site registered, if you want. There are a number of criteria, but, looking through this book, it would appear that the bar is set pretty high. I don't think my house is going to feature. The good people of Unesco, the Unescovites, focus on magical, hugely important places of planetary significance and it is pleasing to see that we have such a generous sprinkling of these in our country.

World Heritage Sites of Britain is both a guide and a reminder. The guide will whisk you from the warm comforts of Bath, to the rugged and bracing island of St Kilda, from the grandeur of Edinburgh to the mysterious bump of Silbury Hill. It will dwell on castle walls and mysterious buried tombs, follow aqueducts and explore botanical gardens (and a very handsome and rewarding guide it is too), but it is as 'a reminder' that this sumptuous book does its finest work. These pages remind us what put the Great in Great Britain.

Tolkien is said to have written *The Lord of the Rings* as a 'Legendorium' to make up a deficiency of proper English myths. Venerating legends as repositories of a higher form of truth, he felt that we lacked a store of ancient old tales and stories, so he famously made one up. But the British do have myths. These are the myths of our own history. We put faith in the achievements of our past and we translate them into the spirit of the nation. The sites here are our latter-day British temples. When I say that they are magical places I mean that they carry a certain power for all true Brits. A true monument is erected to commemorate a great man, but these are monuments to great ideas.

It really doesn't matter that the modern Druidical canon is utter baloney, when we gaze on the great boulders of Stonehenge we experience a shared romance of the Neolithic Age. This is where we British begin, we think, and we may be right. The great buttresses of Welsh castles are the foundation stones of our notion of chivalric heritage. We all know that the Medieval Age actually had little to do with knights and jousting and more to do with three fields and an

ox-drawn plough, but we see the banners of Walter Scott and we imagine ourselves pacing the walls with a tin hat, a lute and a crossbow.

Bath embodies our national, but long lost, elegance, Edinburgh the rigour of our enlightenment, Greenwich the excitement of early science. The places are the stories and the stories make the places. The Tower of London and its Crown Jewels and preposterous Beefeaters are a largely Victorian re-imagining of Merrie England, but that's OK. That romance is part of us. It is an emotional take that we want to commemorate, and here it is, in all its magnificence – something to be proud of. We must preserve our legends. A place, a castle or a town does it for us more emphatically than any academic account could possibly manage. The fading lichen-covered engine houses of Cornish tin mining echo our former true grit and enterprise; Big Pit in Blaenavon our belief in the great Industrial Revolution, with which, we like to imagine, we once led the world. Each of these sites is far more than the sum of its own history.

I am almost ashamed to say that I know a lot of the places rather well. I have canoed under Iron Bridge, strutted up Arthur's Seat, driven a canal boat across the Pontcysyllte Aqueduct (and back again for a second take, when I mucked up the pronunciation). I have strutted in Bath, pontificated at the White Tower and spouted by a tin mine. I have done all these things for a television camera because my producers are no fools. They recognize the mystical power of these places and covet their ability to summon up the ghosts of Britain's past.

The Unescovites are no fools either. These are compelling locations. They deserve their planetary status. And they deserve this book, this guide and this reminder. Let us enjoy and ruminate and go visit, of course.

Griff Rhys Jones

Introduction:
The best on earth

It's a far cry from the elegant, honey-stoned Georgian grandeur of the city of Bath to the wild and remote outer Hebridian islands of St Kilda, thrusting out of the storm-tossed North Atlantic ocean like a set of dragon's teeth. And the contrast between the sumptuous, exotic greenery of the Royal Botanical Gardens at Kew and bleak, wind-blasted Hadrian's Wall in Northumberland, the northernmost outpost of the Roman Empire, could hardly be greater. But all these diverse yet fascinating British landscapes have one thing in common. They all form part of Britain's exclusive collection of World Heritage Sites, designated parts of the world's cultural and natural heritage that are acknowledged to be in possession of 'outstanding universal value' by the World Heritage Committee of the United Nations Educational, Scientific and Cultural Organization (UNESCO).

It was not until 1986 that the first seven British World Heritage Sites were designated. They were the dominating medieval Castles and Town Walls built by King Edward I in Gwynedd, North Wales; Durham's stately Norman Castle and Cathedral; the geological oddities of Giant's Causeway and the Causeway Coast of Antrim, Northern Ireland; the pioneering industrial landscape clustered around the graceful latticework of the Iron Bridge and its gorge in Shropshire; the iconic Neolithic landscapes of Stonehenge and Avebury in Wiltshire; Studley Royal Park, including the evocative ruins of Fountains Abbey, in Yorkshire; and the natural features of that barren and windswept St Kilda archipelago in the Outer Hebrides. (The marine environment surrounding St Kilda was included in 2004, and a year later, the designation was extended to include its cultural history.)

The 305-m (1,000-ft) long and almost unpronounceable Pontcysyllte Aqueduct, which carries the Llangollen Canal 40m (125ft) above the Dee Valley near Wrexham in North Wales was designated in 2009, following the designation of Cornwall and West Devon's tortured tin-mining landscape three years earlier.

All these sites managed to fulfil UNESCO's exacting criteria of 'encouraging the identification, protection and preservation of cultural and natural heritage around the world considered to be of outstanding value to humanity'.

The Abu Simbel story

The idea for providing some kind of international protection for the world's finest natural and cultural sites was born in response to the accelerating pace of destruction that took place during, and in the aftermath of, World War II.

In 1954, international concern was focused on the Nubian temples of the Upper Nile in Egypt. Col. Nasser's government announced it would build the Aswan High Dam and create a vast lake in his name. Supplementing the original Aswan Low Dam, built in 1902, the new dam was needed to regulate the annual flooding of the Nile, to provide water storage for agriculture and, later, to generate hydroelectricity. But the building of the dam would necessitate the flooding of a valley that contained some of the grandest and most beautiful temples of ancient Egypt, including the monumental Abu Simbel and Philae temples.

The Abu Simbel temples were carved directly out of the rock during the reign of Rameses II in the 13th century BC, as a lasting monument to himself and his queen Nefertari. The Great Temple, which consists of four colossal, 20-m (65-ft) high statues of the Pharaoh, took about 20 years to build and was completed in around 1265 BC.

Above: Transporting Abu Simbel block by block in 1966
Right: Sightseers dwarfed by the four enthroned colossi of Rameses
Overleaf: The Merapi volcano from the top of the temple of Borobodur

The temples at Philae, occupying two small islands in the Nile just above the First Cataract, were built during various eras, from the time of the Pharaohs to the Romans. The most ancient was the remains of a temple for the goddess Hathor, built in the reign of Nectanebo I between 380 and 362 BC. Other ruins dated from Ptolemaic times (282–145 BC), with many traces of Roman work.

Faced with the urgent need to save these priceless examples of ancient Egyptian culture, UNESCO launched worldwide 'safeguarding' and international donation campaigns in 1959. The cost of the ambitious and unprecedented Abu Simbel project, which aimed to move the temples physically away from the rising waters of Lake Nasser, was US$80m (£48m), about half of which was eventually collected from 50 countries throughout the world.

The massive operation, described as one of the greatest feats of archaeological engineering ever attempted, took place between 1964 and 1968. The Abu Simbel and Philae temples were taken apart piece by piece, moved to a higher location and put back together like a huge jigsaw. At Abu Simbel, the entire site was cut into large blocks, weighing up to 30 tonnes and averaging 20 tonnes, and reassembled in a new location 65m (213ft) higher and 200m (650ft) back from the river. The Philae temples were reconstructed on an artificial domed hill, high above the rising waters of the reservoir of the Aswan High Dam.

Today, thanks to UNESCO's action, the Abu Simbel and Philae temples remain one of Egypt's top tourist attractions – thousands of visitors flock to see them in their new, artificially constructed sites, some using an airfield specially built for the complex. They are, needless to say, now World Heritage Sites.

The Abu Simbel project was regarded as a huge success, and led to other rescue campaigns: Venice and its lagoon in Italy; the ruins of Mohenjo-daro in Pakistan; and the Borobodur Temple Compounds in the jungles of Indonesia. Eventually, UNESCO, working alongside the International Council on Monuments and Sites, decided it was important to initiate a draft convention 'to protect the world's common cultural heritage for all humanity'.

The WHS Convention

The idea of combining cultural conservation with nature conservation had its genesis in the United States. A White House conference in 1965 called for a 'World Heritage Trust' to preserve 'the world's superb natural and scenic areas and historic sites for the present and the future of the entire world citizenry'. The International Union for Conservation of Nature developed similar proposals in 1968, and they were eventually adopted in 1972 by a United Nations conference on the Human Environment in

Stockholm. A text was agreed by all parties, and the 'Convention Concerning the Protection of the World Cultural and Natural Heritage' was adopted by the General Conference of UNESCO in November 1972.

The nomination process

To nominate a World Heritage Site, a country must first take an inventory of its significant cultural and natural properties on what is called the Tentative List. Next, it can select a property from this list to place into a Nomination File. The World Heritage Centre offers advice and help in preparing this file, and each country can nominate only one site per year for consideration.

At this point, the file is evaluated by the International Council on Monuments and Sites and the World Conservation Union. These bodies then make their recommendations to the World Heritage Committee, which is based in Paris, France.

The World Heritage Committee consists of representatives from 21 of the parties to the Convention, elected by their General Assembly. The committee is responsible for the implementation of the Convention, defines the use of the World Heritage Fund and allocates financial assistance requested by States Parties. It also has the final say on whether a property is 'inscribed' on the World Heritage List. It examines reports on the conservation of inscribed properties and, in cases where it appears that properties are not being properly managed, asks relevant parties to take action. It also decides whether properties on the List of World Heritage in Danger should be inscribed or deleted. The Bureau of the World Heritage Committee is made up of seven representatives elected annually by the Committee: a chair, five vice-chairs and a rapporteur. According to the Convention, a committee member's term of office is for six years, but most parties choose to be members for only four years in order to give others the opportunity to serve on this highly prestigious body.

The Committee meets once a year at different venues throughout the world to determine whether or not to inscribe each nominated property on the World Heritage List. Sometimes it defers the decision to request more information from the country that nominated the site. One such case was the Lake District National Park in Cumbria, which first applied for World Heritage Site status several years ago and is again seeking inscription under a mixed natural and cultural landscape category. It hopes to achieve this by 2012, as do the combined twin Saxon monastic sites of Wearmouth and Jarrow in Tyne and Wear, which also have a well-developed bid.

A similar bid was proposed in 1986 for Creswell Crags, the magnesium limestone gorge on the borders of Derbyshire and Nottinghamshire, where the first examples of rock art in Britain, dating back 13,000 years to the end of the Ice Age, were recently

discovered inside shallow caves. The closure of an adjacent sewage works and the road that used to run through the site, along with the creation of a £6m new museum, education and visitor centre, has renewed optimism in the Creswell Crags bid, which is hoping to get onto the WHS Tentative List as a result.

Selection criteria

There are ten criteria for selection, and a site must meet at least one of them to be included on the list. The criteria, as modified in 2005, cover both the cultural and natural heritage, and nominated sites must fufil that difficult and rather nebulous standard of being of 'outstanding universal value'.

Cultural criteria

To qualify, the proposed site must:

- represent a masterpiece of human creative genius
- exhibit an important interchange of human values, over a span of time or within a cultural area of the world, on developments in architecture or technology, monumental arts, town planning or landscape design
- bear a unique or at least exceptional testimony to a cultural tradition or to a civilization that is living or has disappeared
- be an outstanding example of a type of building, architectural or technological ensemble or landscape that illustrates a significant stage in human history
- be an outstanding example of a traditional human settlement, land use, or sea use which is representative of a culture (or cultures), or human interaction with the environment especially when it has become vulnerable under the impact of irreversible change
- be directly or tangibly associated with events or living traditions, with ideas, or with beliefs, with artistic and literary works of outstanding universal significance. (The Committee considers that this criterion should preferably be used in conjunction with other criteria.)

Natural criteria

The proposed site must:

- contain superlative natural phenomena or areas of exceptional natural beauty and aesthetic importance
- be an outstanding example representing major stages of Earth's history, including the record of life, significant ongoing geological processes in the development of landforms, or significant geomorphic or physiographic features
- be an outstanding example representing significant on-going ecological and biological processes in the evolution and development of terrestrial, freshwater, coastal and marine ecosystems and communities of plants and animals
- contain the most important and significant natural habitats for in-site conservation

of biological diversity, including those containing threatened species of outstanding universal value from the point of view of science or conservation.

The sites

There are currently 890 World Heritage Sites in 148 countries throughout the world. Of these, 689 are categorized for their cultural heritage and 176 for their natural attributes, with 25 exhibiting both cultural and natural features. Italy is home to the greatest number of World Heritage Sites – there are currently 44 on the list. These include the historic cities of Rome, Florence, Venice, Naples and Siena; the archaeologically important sites of Pompei, Herculaneum, Cerveteri and Agrigento, and even whole mountain ranges such as the Dolomites and Bernina Alps.

British World Heritage Sites not featured in this book because of their obvious inaccessibility are the dependencies of Henderson Island in the South Pacific, and Gough and Inaccessible Islands in the South Atlantic.

At the other extreme are the awesome, yawning, mile- (1.6-km) deep vastness of the Grand Canyon in the American West; the sparkling waters of the Great Barrier Reef, that huge coral-crowned breakwater off Australia's east coast; and the man-made ancient wonders and cultural landscapes of the Great Wall of China and the Pyramids and Sphinx of Egypt's Lower Nile Valley. They also include places as unique and diverse as the wildlife wonderlands of East Africa's Serengeti and the baroque cathedrals of Latin America.

In between, there are many, sometimes much more obscure, places that I have been privileged to visit. They include the Head-Smashed-in Buffalo Jump in the Albertan prairies of Canada, where, for nearly 6,000 years until the late 19th century, Blackfoot Indians hunted herds of bison to their deaths over a sandstone escarpment; the site of the world's first-ever parliament at Thingvellir in the centre of Iceland; and the famous rock-cut 'rose red city, half as old as time' at Petra, deep in the recesses of the dusty Jordanian desert. The variety is truly astounding, and you soon realize that it would take many lifetimes to see them all.

You could say that the World Heritage Sites are the jewels in the crown of the world's greatest natural and cultural land- and cityscapes – the places where, if you had to show a visitor from another planet the best of what Earth had to offer, you would take them. Perhaps that's how UNESCO's enigmatic, intergalactic phrase, 'outstanding universal value', came about.

On its website, UNESCO succinctly summarizes the significance of World Heritage Sites: 'Heritage is our legacy from the past, what we live with today, and what we pass

on to future generations. Our cultural and natural heritage are both irreplaceable sources of life and inspiration. 'What makes the concept of World Heritage exceptional is its universal application. World Heritage sites belong to all the peoples of the world, irrespective of the territory on which they are located.'

The British World Heritage Sites

These are listed in order of designation and subsequent adjustments:

- Castles and Town Walls of King Edward I in Gwynedd (1986)
- Durham Castle and Cathedral, Co Durham (1986)
- Giant's Causeway and Causeway Coast, Co Antrim (1986)
- Ironbridge Gorge, Shropshire (1986)
- St Kilda (1986, 2004, 2005)
- Stonehenge, Avebury and Associated Sites, Wiltshire (1986)
- Studley Royal Park including the ruins of Fountains Abbey, Yorkshire (1986)
- Blenheim Palace, Oxfordshire (1987)
- City of Bath, Avon (1987)
- Canterbury Cathedral, St Augustine's Abbey and St Martin's Church, Kent (1987)
- Frontiers of the Roman Empire (Hadrian's and the Antonine Walls) (1987, 2005)
- Westminster Palace, Westminster Abbey and St Margaret's Church, London (1987)
- Tower of London (1988)
- Old and New Towns of Edinburgh (1995)
- Maritime Greenwich, London (1997)
- Heart of Neolithic Orkney (1999)
- Blaenavon Industrial Landscape, Gwent (2000)
- Derwent Valley Mills, Derbyshire (2001)
- Dorset and East Devon Coast (2001)
- New Lanark, Larnarkshire (2001)
- Saltaire, West Yorkshire (2001)
- Royal Botanic Gardens, Kew (2003)
- Liverpool – Maritime Mercantile City (2004)
- Cornwall and West Devon Mining Landscape (2006)
- Pontcysyllte Aqueduct, Llangollen (2009)

Right: The World Heritage emblem, designed by Michel Olyff

The WHS emblem

The distinctive World Heritage emblem, used to identify properties on the official World Heritage List, was adopted as the official logo of the World Heritage Convention in 1978. Designed by Belgian artist Michel Olyff, it represents the universal values for which the Convention, adopted by UNESCO in 1972, stands and the interdependence of the world's natural and cultural diversity.

The central square symbolizes the results of human skill and inspiration, and the circle celebrates the gifts of nature. Like the world, the emblem is round, acting as a symbol of global protection for the heritage of all humankind. The symbol is surrounded by the words 'World Heritage' in three languages: English, French and Spanish.

The West

City of Bath

The ancient city of Bath, synonymous today with honey-stoned Georgian elegance, spreads up in stately, tiered terraces on either side of the River Avon. It is the only complete city in England to be classified a World Heritage Site. Bath gained its designation in 1987 for its 'contribution to urban design, for its architectural quality, its Roman remains, its Georgian town centre and its historic associations'. And the WHS inscription adds: '... last but not least, in spite of all the changes imposed upon it by the 20th century, Bath remains a beautiful city, set in a hollow among hills and as architecturally exciting as it was in its Georgian heyday.'

Modern-day Bath is largely the creation of an aristocratic, foppish young gambler and dedicated follower of fashion Richard Nash, known as Beau Nash, who arrived in the city in 1705. Under his patronage, the city grew quickly and established itself as a highly fashionable spa, where the middle classes of Georgian England could mix with the aristocracy on equal terms in places like the Assembly Rooms and the Pump Room. But the history of Bath goes back much further than that. The Romans were always attracted to warm springs wherever their invading legions marched, and they must have heard about the Bath springs soon after arriving on the south coast of England in AD 43. They were also attracted to the rich resources of galena, or lead ore, found in the neighbouring limestone Mendip Hills. Bath, with its easy exporting route via the Avon to the Bristol Channel, was therefore ideally situated for imperial settlement for several reasons.

Aquae Sulis

The Romans called their grand new city, founded in around AD 63, *Aquae Sulis*, in an astute tribute to the Celtic goddess Sulis, who was worshipped by the local population. The connection with Minerva, the Romans' own goddess of healing, was obvious, so they built their temples to the two deities side by side. The great gorgon, or Green Man-like, stone head of Sul-Minerva – all bulging, staring eyes and writhing, serpent-like beard and hair – forms the centrepiece of the modern visitor complex. The head, which is a vigorous masterpiece cleverly combining Roman and Celtic beliefs in its representation of both goddesses, was discovered during the building of the Pump Room in 1790. It is thought to have formed the centrepiece of the pediment of the Roman temple, flanked by winged Victories. The Romans took the sacred Celtic site and transformed it into one of the first British spas – an international attraction to which toga-clad dignitaries flocked from all over the Empire to enjoy its curative waters. The Roman writer Solinus described Bath as the most excellent town in Roman Britain, 'furnished luxuriously for human use'.

Above top: Richard 'Beau' Nash, the dandy associated with Bath, when somewhat past his prime...
Bottom: Gorgon's Head from the pediment of the Temple of Sulis Minerva

Some of the 1,900-year-old Roman engineering survives to this day, including the vast reservoir lined with Mendip lead, which encloses the main warm water spring. The water still gushes impressively out of the rock at over one million litres (240,000 gallons) a day and at an average temperature of 46° C (115° F).

The Great Bath, also lined with Mendip lead, can still be seen, along with its built-in seating for bathers and its green, slightly steaming waters. The colonnades and statues around the baths are later reconstructions. The Roman baths, together with the *tepidarium* (warm room), *caldarium* (hot room) and even a *laconium* (hot, dry room, like a modern sauna), were open to both sexes and formed the centre of the social life of *Aquae Sulis* for close on 300 years, just as they did for Beau Nash 1,300 years later. The baths were constantly improved and extended during the Roman period, but after the Romans left in around AD 400, they fell into disrepair, as an eight-century chronicler recorded in his poem 'The Ruin':

Wondrous is this stone-wall, wrecked by fate;
the city-buildings crumble, the work of giants decay.
Roofs have caved in, towers collapsed,
barred gates are broken, hoar frost clings to mortar,
houses are gaping, tottering and fallen,
undermined by age. The earth's embrace,
its fierce grip, holds the mighty craftsmen;
they are perished and gone. A hundred generations
have passed away since then. This wall, grey with lichen
and red of hue, outlives kingdom after kingdom,
withstands tempests; its tall gate succumbed.
The city still moulders, gashed by storms…

Despite this, Bath must have still been important in Anglo-Saxon times: Edgar, nephew of Edward the Elder, was crowned king of all England on Whit Sunday, AD 973, at the Anglo-Saxon Benedictine abbey that had been constructed using masonry from the former Roman city. Edgar was successful in uniting the various kingdoms of England, and his Bath ceremony set the format for all subsequent British coronations.

In Norman times, Bath took over from Wells as the seat of the bishopric of Somerset. The abbey was raised to the status of cathedral and dedicated to St Peter and St Paul. Over time, the cathedral fell into disrepair until Bishop Oliver King instigated a programme of rebuilding in the early 16th century (see box, p.27). Later, the seat returned to Wells; the modern bishopric covers both Bath and Wells. Bishop King employed the royal master masons Robert and William Vertue, who were later to work on St George's Chapel, Windsor, and Westminster Abbey. They promised to create

'the finest vault in England' but, by the time of the Dissolution of the Monasteries, only the magnificent west front, the walls and part of the choir were completed. After the Dissolution, the fine Gothic building was stripped of its lead and looted. During Bath's glamorous Georgian heyday, it stood unloved and ruinous, with only the choir used for services. The long-awaited restoration by George Gilbert Scott did not take place until 1864, when he virtually rebuilt the nave and aisles, meticulously replicating Bishop King's fan vaulting and buttresses, and restoring the famous west front with its angels ascending the 'stairway to heaven' (see box, left). For the most part, what we see today at Bath Abbey is actually a Victorian replica of a Tudor design, but it remains a faithful copy. Even in its rebuilt and heavily restored Victorian state, Bath Abbey has been called 'the grandest parish church in England'.

Fashionable spa

Bath's days of fame and glory during the Georgian period can be traced back to a visit by Queen Anne in 1702–3 to take the waters. Hot on her heels came her court and its fashionable followers, most notably Beau Nash, who was appointed 'Master of Ceremonies'. It was Nash who tore down the elaborate protocols that had excluded all but the upper classes, and it was he who transformed the city into a fashionable spa. After Dr William Oliver – inventor of the Bath Oliver biscuit – had built the first Mineral Water Hospital in 1740, Nash used the father-and-son team of John Wood the elder and younger as the chief architects to transform the largely medieval city into the elegant Bath we see today. Most notable among their many achievements were the sweeping lines of The Royal Crescent (1767–75), whose Ionic columns are so often used as a backdrop to television and film costume dramas; the Assembly Rooms (1771), gutted by a Luftwaffe Baedeker air raid in 1942 but now handsomely restored; and the beautiful circle of King's Circus (1754), which consists of 30 houses adorned by a classical succession of Doric, Ionic and Corinthian columns. King's Circus was once thought to have been modelled on the Roman Colosseum but now it is generally believed that Wood the elder based its dimensions on the Neolithic stone circles at nearby Stanton Drew and Stonehenge. Wood was fascinated by the druids, and masonic symbols are carved above the first row of pillars, along with acorns around the parapet, which recall the legend of Bladud, the legendary founder of the city (see box, p.28). Lansdown Crescent, which some people find even more aesthetically pleasing than the more famous Royal Crescent, was designed and built by John Palmer between 1789 and 1793. It still retains the ironwork overhead lamps across the porches to its fan-headed doors. A famous former resident at No. 19 was the eccentric writer William Beckford, who lived here from 1822. He was responsible for the folly known as Beckford's Tower, a recently restored, narrow, lantern-topped structure on the hills above the town.

Left: Bath Abbey and the entrance to the Roman Baths and Pump Rooms

THE BALLAD OF BLADUD

The legendary founder of the city of Bath was Bladud, father of Lud Hudibras, who has been identified with Shakespeare's mad monarch King Lear. Legend states that Prince Bladud was banished from court because he suffered from leprosy and could not return home until he was cured. Another story says he spent 11 years in Athens, where he contracted the disease. On returning home still with leprosy, Bladud found work as a lowly swineherd in the village of Swainswick, about 3 miles (4.8km) north of the present city. One day, he noticed that his pigs were wallowing in a black, evil-smelling bog fed by warm springs. The hot water and mud seemed to cure the pigs of the scurf and scabs on their hides. Bladud thought he'd give the water a try on his leprous skin and dived into the mire with his pigs. Lo and behold, he was cured and became the first beneficiary of Bath's healing waters. Socially acceptable once more, the now smooth-skinned Bladud became the ninth King of the Britons in 863 BC, and founded the city of Bath on the River Avon near the health-giving springs. He called it *Caer Badon*, or the fortress of the baths.

The Pump Room was designed by Thomas Baldwin and built between 1786 and 1792. Here you can still taste the pungent, mineral-rich waters – famously described by Sam Weller in Dickens's *The Pickwick Papers* as tasting like 'warm flat irons' – watched over by a statue of Beau Nash and to the accompaniment of the Pump Room String Trio, the oldest established musical ensemble in Britain.

One of the most famous views in the city of Bath is that of the crescent-shaped weir in the River Avon below the three beautifully proportioned arches of Pulteney Bridge. This handsome structure was designed by Robert Adam and built in 1770 for the landowner Robert, Lord Pulteney, to allow access to his planned village of Bathwick across the river. Like the old London Bridge or Florence's Ponte Vecchio, Pulteney Bridge was designed to have small shops ranged along its length.

Just outside Bath and with stunning panoramic views across the city is the porticoed Palladian mansion of Prior Park, designed by John Wood the elder for quarrymaster Ralph Allen in 1735. Described by the architectural historian Pevsner as 'the most ambitious and the most complete re-creation of Palladio's villas on English soil', it is now a private college, but the 28-acre gardens, landscaped by Alexander Pope and 'Capability' Brown, are in the hands of the National Trust. The highlights of the gardens include an elegant Palladian bridge, built in 1750 as an 'eye-catcher' spanning the serpentine lake and a direct copy of the more famous one at Wilton House, near Salisbury; a Gothic temple; a grotto named after Allen's wife; and a sham castle, which Allen could see from his town house in the centre of Bath.

Above: An 1820 engraving of Lansdown Crescent
Right: Pulteney Bridge, floodlit at night

Cornwall & West Devon Mining Landscape

Where there's a mine or a hole in the ground
That's what I'm heading for, that's where I'm found,
So look for me under the lode and inside the vein.
Where the copper, the clay, the arsenic and tin
Run in your blood and under your skin
I'll leave the county behind, I'm not coming back
Follow me down cousin Jack.

From the song 'Cousin Jack' by Steve Knightley, Show of Hands

As it says in Steve Knightley's song about Cornish miners – colloquially and collectively known as 'Cousin Jack' – it's a pretty safe bet that wherever in the world you peer into a mine, the chances are you'll find a Cornishman. The extraordinary story of the wholesale Cornish and west Devon migration of miners is inextricably linked to the rise and subsequent decline of the region's tin- and copper-mining industry. Skilled miners had been migrating to other parts of Britain from the 1700s, but this was merely a taste of things to come. In the early 1800s, the mining region of Cornwall and west Devon possessed the best contemporary European mining knowledge, with its miners reckoned to be among the world's greatest, and it had begun to export both its technology and labour.

When the tin and copper mines started to fail in the mid-1800s, many Cornishmen and women emigrated to the mining frontiers of North America and other far-flung places. Cornishmen were among the earliest prospectors in the Klondike and Californian gold rushes in the 19th century. According to Thomas A. Rickard, writing in *A History of American Mining* (1932), Cornishmen 'knew better than anyone how to break rock, how to timber bad ground, and how to make the other fellow shovel it, tram it and hoist it'. They also took part in the Witwatersrand gold rush in the Transvaal of South Africa, and the gold rushes in New Zealand and Brazil.

The most significant exodus of people took place in the period known as the Great Migration between 1815 and 1930, when Cornwall lost some 20 per cent of its adult male population overseas in every decade between 1861 and 1901 – three times the national average. It was an emigration comparable to the great diaspora caused by the Irish Potato Famine. Today, there are reckoned to be over six million people of Cornish descent throughout the world.

During the Bronze Age, between 2000 and 1000 BC, Phoenician traders from the eastern Mediterranean are known to have visited the rocky coasts of Cornwall in search of tin – an essential component of bronze. It was such an important commodity for these traders that they named Britain the Cassiterides, or Tin Islands, and they exchanged pottery, wine, olives and other luxury goods for the precious ore.

The Greek historian Diodorus Siculus, writing in the first century BC, described ancient tin mining in Britain: 'They that inhabit the British promontory of Balerion (modern Cornwall) by reason of their converse with strangers are more civilized and courteous to strangers than the rest are. These are the people that prepare the tin, which with a great deal of care and labour, they dig out of the ground, and that being done the metal is mixed with some veins of earth out of which they melt the metal and refine it. Then they cast it into regular blocks and carry it to a certain island near at hand called Ictis for at low tide, all being dry between there and the island, tin in large quantities is brought over in carts.'

Several locations have been suggested for '*Ictis*', which means 'tin port', including St Michael's Mount but, as a result of extensive research and excavation, archaeologist and Celtic scholar Barry Cunliffe has proposed that it's likely to have been Mount Batten above Plymouth harbour.

Cornwall and the far west of Devon provided the majority of the UK's tin, copper and arsenic for centuries. Originally the tin was found as alluvial deposits in the gravel of stream beds but eventually underground working took place, with the first mines sunk as early as the 16th century. Tin was also dug out from lodes in cliff outcrops.

The scene today

It is the tortured former mining landscape of Cornwall and west Devon – a fascinating area characterized by smelting chimneys, quarries and disturbed ground – that led to its designation as a World Heritage Site in 2006. Any walker along the South West Coast Path National Trail, especially around St Just-in-Penwith and St Agnes, cannot fail to notice the tell-tale chimneys teetering on the edge of the rugged coast, with the mighty waves of the Atlantic crashing into the granite cliffs below.

Among the most accessible tin-mining sites near St Just is the Levant Mine, restored by the National Trust, which houses the oldest beam engine in Cornwall and is still powered by steam. Here you can follow ex-miners underground and view the winding and pumping shafts, which drained the shafts that went out under the Atlantic for over a mile (1.6km). A short walk along the cliffs from the Levant Mine is Botallack Count House (also National Trust). This was the account house for the mining

Left: Artist's impression of Portreath Mine, 1907
Overleaf: The ruins of Botallack Tin Mine engine
house on the cliffs near St Just

company, where the miners received their hard-earned weekly pay packets. Near by, too, is Geevor Mine, the second-to-last tin mine in Cornwall to be finally abandoned in 1991. It is now the Geevor Tin Mine Museum and Heritage Site, where you can view many authentic mining exhibits, including the evocative Miner's Dry building, complete with original lockers and ephemera. For a taste of what life was like for the 18th-century tin miners, you can actually enter the former Wheal Mexico mine.

The area between Gwennap with Devoran and Kennall Vale contains extensive remains of old copper mines and shafts, and was once described as 'the richest square mile in the Old World' due to the huge amount of ore extracted here. One of the most impressive sites here is the Gwennap Pit. This deep, grassy depression, caused by mining subsidence, was used as an open-air preaching venue by the likes of John Wesley, the methodist minister, who visited the pit on no fewer than 18 occasions between 1776 and 1789. Located just to the south of Redruth, the 13 rows of terraces in the depression walls were cut by miners to create seating, and an annual Whit Monday Methodist service has been held here since 1807. The green amphitheatre of Gwenapp Pit has also been used for Chartist meetings and theatrical performances. You might well recognize the picturesque harbour and quay at Charlestown, just off the A38 west of Plymouth, because it has served as the period backdrop to countless films, television programmes and advertisements. The harbour, where you'll often find four-masted sailing ships moored, was built by John Smeaton at the end of the 18th century for the export of both copper ore and china clay. Near by is the impressive, ten-arched Treffry Viaduct, built in 1839–42 to cross the Luxulyan Valley by Joseph Teffry, who owned the Fowey Consuls Mine.

Another busy port that exported tin and copper was Morwellham Quay, 4 miles (6.4km) south of Tavistock. Copper was brought from the nearby William & Mary Mine and the George & Charlotte Mine, named after the 18th-century monarchs and their consorts. You can still see the water wheels, tramways and kilns used by those early miners. Today, Morwellham Quay has a thriving visitor centre, with a fascinating museum. Across the large green stands a terrace of spacious houses built by William Russell, 7th Duke of Bedford, to house his workers. Morwellham is linked to the town of Tavistock and its mines by the 4-mile (6.4-km) long Tavistock Canal.

The largest mine in the area was the Devon Great Consuls near Tavistock. It was also once the richest copper mine in Europe, and the supplier of most of the world's arsenic. The town of Tavistock was the beneficiary of all this wealth, and the Duke of Bedford bequeathed many fine public buildings to the town. His statue still looks out over the town square. Other important landowners included the Godolphin family, who made their fortune from the rich tin deposits on their estate near Helston. Sir William Godolphin, a soldier in the service of Henry VIII, was comptroller of the

Left: Miners working underground at Geevor Mine in the 1930s

coinage of tin (as the tax payable to the crown was known) and sheriff of the county of Cornwall, and his son was appointed Master of the Mines. The originally Tudor family home of Godolphin House stands in glorious isolation amid the 550-acre estate and historically important gardens, owned by the National Trust since 2000.

Granite-built Godolphin is one of Cornwall's most beautiful houses. In the 17th century, when Italian classicism was making its first appearance in England, it was considered the most fashionable house in the county. In 1630, Sir Francis Godolphin had the north front redesigned as a unique double open arcade; the upper floor is carried on eight Tuscan columns, repeated on the other side of a screen wall. Over-enthusiastic local masons topped off the parapet with a distinctly unclassical-looking battlement, before work was finally brought to a halt by the Civil War. The future Charles II took refuge at Godolphin in 1646 as he fled to the Scilly Isles, where the royalist sympathizer Sir Francis Godolphin, who accompanied him, was Governor. But the family rose again in importance following the Restoration, when Sidney, 1st Earl of Godolphin became Queen Anne's Lord Treasurer in 1702. However, after 1710 no Godolphins lived here, and the house and estate fell slowly into disrepair. It could be said that Godolphin encapsulates the entire 4,000-year history of the Cornwall and west Devon mining landscape. Along the many interesting walks on the estate you can see more than 400 recorded archaeological features, including 19th-century tin-mining remains at the Goldolphin Mine, and hut circles dating from the Bronze Age, when Cornish tin first hit the world market.

Above: Tall ship moored in Charlestown harbour
Right: Inside Godolphin House

Dorset & East Devon Coast – the Jurassic Coast

Unlike the unfortunate family in Steven Spielberg's 1993 blockbuster *Jurassic Park*, you won't be attacked by velociraptors as you walk along the spectacular Jurassic Coast of Dorset and East Devon. But if you look carefully, you could well find the fossilized bones of their cousins. With just a smattering of knowledge about the rocks beneath your feet, you can be transported back through 180 million years of geological history, to the very dawn of life on Earth. The varied geology of the Dorset and East Devon Coast has been described as a unique, beautifully exposed outdoor laboratory for the study of the rocks, the shape of the land and the processes that created them.

The story of the Jurassic Coast begins when the rocks were laid down in the far-off Mesozoic era – which means the 'Middle Ages' – of life on Earth. The Mesozoic era is made up of three distinct periods of geological time – the Triassic, the Jurassic and the Cretaceous – all of which are represented in the 95-mile (155-km) long World Heritage coastline that runs between Exmouth in East Devon to the west, and Old Harry Rocks near Poole in Dorset to the east. The World Heritage designation – the first natural site to be so recognized in Britain – was made in 2001, in an acknowledgment of the unique and virtually continuous sequence of Mesozoic rocks that are exposed, plus the internationally important fossil deposits that have been found here since the days of the earliest prospector, Mary Anning (see box, right).

Understanding the rocks: a piece of cake

The best way to understand the sequence of rocks that you encounter along the Jurassic Coast is to imagine a layer cake with alternate fillings and cake mix, with the oldest layers at the bottom of the 'cake' and the youngest on the top. The oldest and lowest layers in the Jurassic Coast date from the Triassic period, between 200 and 250 million years ago. The next layers are from the fossil-rich Jurassic period, about 140 million years ago. Finally, you have the Cretaceous layers, dating from 70 million years ago. Now picture the 'layer cake' turned on its side to the right, so that all the rocks are standing upright, with the oldest (the Triassic) at the western (left) end of the coast between Exmouth to Pinhay Bay; the Jurassic in the middle, roughly between Lyme Regis and Durlston Head; and the Cretaceous at the eastern end, between Osmington and Old Harry Rocks to the south of Poole Harbour. Cataclysmic earth movements over many millions of years caused this up-turning of the Dorset coast 'layer cake', to give us the vertical, upstanding sequence of rocks we see today. Of course, this contorted confection is a highly simplified explanation, and there are

important inliers of Cretaceous rocks in the Triassic layer between Branscombe and Beer, and the older Jurassic rocks are exposed in the Cretaceous layer at Lulworth Cove and between Kimmeridge and Durlston Head.

As you stand on the dramatic, windswept, rusty-red cliffs of Orcombe Point, which marks the western end of the World Heritage Site, it's hard to imagine that if you'd been here when the rocks were laid down, you would have experienced the blistering heat of a baking, arid desert like the modern Sahara. When these Triassic rocks were deposited over 200 million years ago, this part of Britain was much closer to the equator and in a desert environment of sand dunes, salt lakes, lagoons and rivers. The rusty-reds and oranges of the cliffs are due to the weathering of iron minerals within the rocks, and are a sure sign for geologists that these rocks were formed in hot, desert conditions.

A walk around Orcombe Point at low tide reveals the cross-bedded sandstones that formed in rivers due to the actions of currents on the sand. During dry periods, sand was blown out from the riverbeds to form dunes in the neighbouring East Devon desert. The shapely Geoneedle, which tops the cliffs at Orcombe Point, was unveiled by the Prince of Wales in 2002, when he inaugurated the World Heritage Site. It is constructed from the major building stones found along the Jurassic Coast. Just to the west of Budleigh Salterton's sea front lie the famous Budleigh Salterton Pebble Beds, eroded out from the adjacent cliffs. These incredibly ancient, 440-million-year-old quartzite pebbles are thought to have come from what is modern Brittany,

Above right: Ammonite fossil from the Cretaceous period
Overleaf: The cliff face of East Devon's stunning Heritage Coastline

transported by one of the huge rivers that flowed into the Triassic desert about 240 million years ago. The larger quartzite pebbles are very hard and constitute the oldest rocks anywhere along the Heritage Coast. Their hardness meant that they survived being transported along the coast by longshore drift, and they can be found all along the Channel coast, from Slapton Sands in Devon to Hastings in Kent. The beach at Budleigh Salterton is made almost entirely of these ancient pebbles, but other beaches on the coast, such as that at Beer, are made mainly from flint and chert, which has been eroded out from the chalk cliffs. These are the youngest rocks on the Heritage Coast. The fishing village of Beer (the name has nothing to do with a local brew but is an old Devon word for grove) is beautifully situated in a bay sheltered by dazzlingly white chalk cliffs. These crumbly rocks were formed from the remains of millions of tiny sea creatures that lived in the shallow subtropical seas covering this part of East Devon in the Cretaceous period, over 70 million years ago.

Lyme Regis and The Undercliff

The Saxon harbour town of Lyme gained the suffix 'Regis' in 1284 when Edward I granted it a royal charter. No fewer than five ships sailed from The Cobb, Lyme's famous sickle-shaped breakwater, to fight the Spanish Armada in 1588. But the town owes its more recent fame to appearances in the novels *Persuasion* by Jane Austen and *The French Lieutenant's Woman* by John Fowles, which was made into a successful film starring Meryl Streep and Jeremy Irons in 1981. Today, Lyme Regis is full of curio and fossil shops, which attract the rockhound, while the Dinosaurland Fossil Museum has among its exhibits some of the more notable prehistoric reptiles found in the area, as well as a 73-kg (160-lb) lump of dinosaur dung. Just to the east of Lyme Regis stands the bold headland of Golden Cap. At 188m (616ft), it is the highest point on the south coast of England. This beautiful National Trust property gets its name from the cap of golden sandstone that tops the cliff face.

The journey on the South West Coast Path between Axmouth and Lyme Regis is one of the toughest and most strenuous sections of the 595-mile (958-km) National Trail. The whole area forms the Undercliffs National Nature Reserve, one of the most important wilderness areas in southern Britain. The entire reserve is formed from landslides, and is particularly famous for the enormous one that took place at Bindon in 1839 (see box, right). The Jurassic Coast is prone to such landslides, and there are many historical records of them here, dating back to the 17th century. They are still occurring today, creating an internationally important mix of habitats, from dense scrub and woodland to open ground, with many specially adapted plants and animals. Natural England manages the reserve, and visitors are required to keep to the path that runs through it. The rocks making up the Jurassic cliffs at Charmouth are rich in the fossils of creatures that once swam in the primordial seas. The coast here is eroding rapidly, resulting in thousands of fossils being left on the beaches after

WHEN THE EARTH MOVED: THE BINDON LANDSLIDE

The Bindon Landslide, which took place on the Undercliff to the west of Lyme on Christmas Day in 1839, attracted national publicity and thousands of visitors. A huge piece of land, known locally as Goat Island because goats were once grazed on it, slipped towards the sea as the shales gave way, leaving a deep chasm between it and the cliffs behind.

The front edge of the landslide was lifted out of the sea, forming a mile- (1.6-km) long natural reef and harbour. Although it proved to be a short-lived feature, questions were asked in Parliament about whether it could become a port for the Navy, perhaps rivalling nearby Poole Harbour.

People flocked to see the landslide by paddle steamer in special excursions from Weymouth and Lyme Regis, and many beautiful prints and engravings were made of the scene. The following August, thousands of people, including the young Queen Victoria, came to see the harvesting of a wheatfield that had been bodily transported by the landslide. Perhaps uniquely among geological events, it had a piece of music and dance, the 'Landslide Quadrille', composed to commemorate it. The 1839 event, technically known as a blockslide, was also notable because two eminent scientists, William Conybeare, then vicar of Axminster, and William Buckland, professor of Geology at Oxford, used it to make the first truly scientific description of a landslide.

landslides from the surrounding cliffs, especially after winter storms. These remains, which have been found here since the 18th century, are said to represent one of the richest slices of life in Jurassic times anywhere in the world. You need sharp eyesight to discover fossils among the rocks and pebbles on the beach, and the best time to go 'fossicking' is when the tide is falling. Common finds include spiral ammonites, so-called 'thunderbolt' belemnites and, if you are really lucky, a fragment of dinosaur bone. A recent important discovery on this part of the coast was the almost complete 3-m (10-ft) long skeleton of a 195 million-year-old scelidosaurus, the earliest of the armoured dinosaurs and a species thought to be unique to this location.

Pebble heaven

It's claimed that on foggy nights in the past, local smugglers coming ashore on the 17-mile (28-km) long beach at Chesil could tell exactly where they were from the size of the pebbles underfoot. This is because the size of the pebbles increases, as does the height of the beach, as you travel eastwards. Thus at West Bay, near Bridport, the pebbles are the size of peas, while at the identically named West Bay at the eastern end of the now 15m- (50-ft) high beach in the shadow of Portland Bill, they can reach the size of a large baking potato. The pebbles – there are said to be 180 billion of them in the 160-m (525-ft) wide beach – are constantly in motion, moving inexorably east along the beach, driven by the action of the wind and waves in a phenomenon known as longshore drift. The apparent east–west grading of the pebbles is thought to have come about because the larger pebbles move faster than smaller ones as the waves wash over them.

Chesil Beach is Britain's finest tombolo (a beach joining two pieces of land) and one of the best examples of a barrier beach in the world. It has stood up to the full force of Channel gales for thousands of years, providing a constant breakwater and protection for the Fleet Lagoon lying behind it. Covering 1,200 acres, the Fleet – the largest tidal lagoon in Britain – is a place of international importance for birds and marine wildlife, and includes the famous Abbotsbury Swannery. This is said to be the oldest managed swan population in the world, and you can watch as up to 600 of these regal birds are fed daily.

The stone that built London

The next great landmark on the Heritage Coast is the bold limestone headland known as the Isle of Portland. It is, however, not an island at all but joined to the mainland by a narrow isthmus of land used by the A354 from Weymouth. The Isle of Portland is the unique source of the fine white limestone known as Portland stone, one of the most famous building stones in the world. The Romans were the first to use it, notably at their regional capital at *Durnovaria* (modern Dorchester), nearly 2,000 years ago. Interestingly, the Romans marked their stone blocks with a series of

cuts to denote volume, and similar marks were still in use in the 1950s. The earliest quarries were those at Tout, where contemporary sculptures can be seen, and at Kingbarrow, which were created as the quarrymen worked the stone along huge natural fractures (gullies), depositing the waste behind them. This creates a strange, slightly North Country type of landscape with drystone walls, tracks and quarry faces. Over the centuries, Portland stone has been used for many of London's finest and most important buildings: the original Palace of Westminster in 1347, the Tower of London in 1349, the first stone London Bridge in 1350 and, later, St Paul's Cathedral, Buckingham Palace, the Bank of England, the British Museum and the Cenotaph in Whitehall. The headquarters of the United Nations in New York are also built of Portland stone.

Dorset's Texas

East of Weymouth, which owes its fame to the royal patronage of George III in the late 18th century, the World Heritage coast is a complex sequence of Upper Jurassic clays, limestones and sandstones. The coast around Osmington is famous because of a natural seepage of oil rising from a breach in an undersea reservoir. On a calm day, oil can sometimes be seen seeping onto the surface of the sea near Bran Point, between Osmington Mills and the deserted medieval village of Ringstead. The oil is held in the layer of rock known as Cornbrash limestone, which can also be found at Kimmeridge, east of Lulworth. BP's 'nodding donkey' on the cliff top at Kimmeridge has been pumping oil for 50 years. The oil formed in rocks that were once the floor of a deep, tropical sea, rich in life in the Jurassic period, around 155 million years ago. The rocks were buried and organic matter within them created the oil and gas fields. More oil lies in the northern part of Purbeck and under Poole Harbour, where the Wytch Farm Oilfield is the largest onshore oil field in the country. The massive cliff at White Nothe, east of Ringstead, consists of Cretaceous chalk and sandstone, on top of Jurassic clays. A landslide in 1826 created the phenomenon known as the Burning Cliff, when a chemical reaction caused the organic-rich clays to start smouldering.

The wonders of Lulworth

The most famous and photographed features on this World Heritage coast are grouped near the perfect scallop-shell bay of Lulworth Cove. Walking along the coast path from the west, and crossing a dry valley with the amusing name of Scratchy Bottom, the first stunning feature you come across is the natural flying buttress known as Durdle Door. This limestone spur has almost been destroyed by the action of the waves, but the soaring arch still stands as an example of differential erosion. Near by is the celebrated Lulworth Crumple, exhibited by the contorted, upturned limestones of Stair Hole. This complex fold, which tilted the rocks so that they are now almost vertical, took place after catastrophic earth movements, which also formed the Alps. In a few million years' time, Stair Hole will be a bay like nearby Lulworth, created when a stream breached the limestone barrier, allowing the sea to enter and hollow out the softer clays lying behind it against the resistant chalk cliffs at the back of the bay. Lulworth is visited by thousands of people every year, and there is a visitor centre and exhibition provided by the Lulworth Estate at the Cove. What is claimed to be the most complete fossil record of a Jurassic forest in the world can be seen to the east of Lulworth Cove, on a wide ledge in the cliff. The site between Lulworth and Kimmeridge lies within army ranges, so is subject to restricted opening times.

Cliffs and quarries

The sheer cliffs of the south Purbeck coast offer some of the most spectacular coastal walking in Britain. Formed of Portland and Purbeck limestone, the rocks are exposed in the former cliff quarry workings of Seacombe, Winspit and Dancing Ledge. The limestone downland beyond supports internationally important plants and animals, while the cliffs are home to colonies of breeding sea birds. Hard-wearing Purbeck limestone has been in demand since Roman times. The quality of the stone varies from layer to layer, making it suitable for a range of uses, from ornamental columns to paving stones. Purbeck limestone produces a uniquely important record of mammal evolution from the dawn of the Cretaceous period. Small, shrew-sized creatures lived at the fringes of lagoons in waterlogged marshland around 140 million years ago. It also contains fossils of reptiles and amphibians, and a total of more than 100 different vertebrate species have been identified. Among the most famous fossil traces in the Purbeck limestones are dinosaur tracks, mostly of megalosaurs and iguanodons. In 1986, footprints over 1m (3ft) in diameter – probably made by a large, plant-eating dinosaur such as a diplodocus – were found in Keats Quarry.

The World Heritage Site reaches its easternmost terminus just beyond the great chalk headland of Ballard Down and the isolated sea stacks off Handfast Point, known as Old Harry Rocks. On a clear day, the similar chalk stacks of the Needles on the Isle of Wight are visible – it is thought that at one time they were connected to Ballard Down. The superb downland habitat, rich in plantlife and butterflies such as the chalkhill and Adonis blue, is owned by the National Trust.

Old Harry Rocks vividly show the dramatic effects of wave erosion. The constant battering of the waves attacks the weak joints in the rock to form arches and caves, which eventually collapse, leaving isolated stacks. There was once a smaller sea stack known as Old Harry's Wife, but it fell victim to the waves about 50 years ago. Who was Old Harry? One story claims that the rocks were named after a famous Poole pirate called Harry Paye, who stored his contraband nearby. Another claims that the Devil (sometimes known as Old Harry) slept on the rocks. The large outcrop at the end of the cliff is often referred to as No Man's Land, and it would indeed take a brave man like *Jurassic Park*'s Alan Grant (played by Sam Neill) to visit it.

Right: Old Harry Rocks

Stonehenge, Avebury & Associated Sites

Forty years ago, the eminent archaeologist Jacquetta Hawkes, wife of novelist and playwright J.B. Priestley, famously suggested: 'Every age has the Stonehenge it deserves – or desires.' Certainly, there has never been any shortage of theories about the whys, whens and wherefores of Britain's most iconic prehistoric monument, which was made a World Heritage Site with Avebury and their associated sites in 1986.

In the Middle Ages, it was thought that Stonehenge had been built by giants. Geoffrey of Monmouth claimed in his *History of the Kings of Britain* (c.1136) that the Giant's Dance rocks on Mount Killaraus in Ireland, originally transported by giants from Africa, were erected by Arthur's mentor, the wizard Merlin, to mark the victory of the Romano-British war leader Aurelius Ambrosius over the Saxons near Amesbury.

There's even a famous illustration from a 14th-century manuscript showing a gigantic Merlin towering over astonished onlookers and blithely popping a Stonehenge lintel onto its uprights.

During the Renaissance, Inigo Jones, James I's architect and Surveyor of the King's Works, equated Stonehenge's regular trilithons and precise measurements with the classical Palladian architecture of Rome, and attributed its building to the imperial forces during their 400-year occupation of Britain. Jones's detailed, symmetrical 1652 plan of Stonehenge was even later used as the blueprint for John Nash's Regency Circus in Bath, another future World Heritage Site. The much-travelled Phoenicians and Danes have also been cited as possible builders.

In the 17th century, antiquarians, like local Wiltshire man John Aubrey, were sure Stonehenge was the work of the druidical 'Ancient Britons', and it was Aubrey who first discovered the eponymous Aubrey Holes, a ring of 56 pits just inside the perimeter bank of the monument. He thought they once held more stones, but later excavation proved they were burial pits for cremations. Aubrey also seems to have been the first to notice Avebury and its enormous henge enclosing twin stone circles, which dwarf those at Stonehenge and encompass the whole village.

Aubrey's meticulous fieldwork and surveying of the site was continued by the young Lincolnshire doctor William Stukeley, the first secretary of the Society of Antiquaries. Stukeley spent several summers at Stonehenge and Avebury between 1721 and 1724, surveying, measuring and drawing, and producing some beautiful views of the entire Stonehenge landscape, which are still admired and referred to by archaeologists today. He agreed with Aubrey, concluding that the whole complex was an elaborate temple used by druids. These mystical rulers and priests of the Ancient Britons were ethnically cleansed by Suetonius Paulinus and his invading Roman army on the island of Anglesey in AD 60. The druids were a sect for which Stukeley had long held a great affection; he even styled himself 'Chyndonax, Prince of the Druids', taking the name of a French druid.

White-robed, modern-day druids still congregate in great numbers around the stone circle every summer solstice – the longest day of the year. With a generous dispensation from Stonehenge's current managers, English Heritage, they are allowed inside the perimeter fence to touch the stones, a privilege denied ordinary visitors for many years. The visitor facilities at Britain's premier prehistoric monument have long been described as 'a national disgrace', with visitors approaching the iconic stones via a rather squalid tunnel under the A344. Until June 2010, construction work had been about to start on new facilities, scheduled to open in time for the London Olympics, when tourist numbers to the site were expected to soar. However, spending cutbacks

announced by the new coalition government put paid to these plans. It seems that we will have to wait a little longer for that 'national disgrace' to be rectified.

By Victorian times, Stonehenge and its associated monuments were attracting the attention of artists. Memorable depictions of the famous site were made by JMW Turner and John Constable – Turner in a melodramatic but popular painting and print of 1828, where a bolt of lightning has struck lifeless a flock of sheep and their unfortunate shepherd, and Constable in his equally storm-tossed and rainbow-washed vision of 1835. Writing in *Antiquity* magazine in 1967, at the dawning of the computer age, Jacquetta Hawkes commented that our greatest prehistoric monument appeared to have been taken over by astronomers and regarded as a celestial observatory and calculating machine by people like Professors Gerald Hawkins and Fred Hoyle.

In the more mystical New Age of the late 1980s, it was argued that the monument was really a spaceport for aliens and UFOs, and the preponderance of crop circles in the area was used as 'evidence' to back up this hypothesis. A gynaecologist from the University of British Columbia has even claimed recently that it was a giant fertility symbol, constructed in the shape of the female sexual organ. We are still, it seems, getting the Stonehenge we deserve.

How it was built

It's been estimated that Stonehenge took around 700 years, starting in around 2200 BC, to build in all its various phases – roughly the same time as Westminster Abbey,

How the internal ring of 45 spotted dolerite bluestones each weighing 4 tonnes got to Stonehenge from the Preseli Mountains of north Pembrokeshire 240 miles (380km) away is a question that has plagued archaeologists for 150 years. Among the more fanatastic theories was that the stones were transported as erratics by Ice Age glaciers. However, there is no evidence of any glaciation covering the area that could have carried them and left no other trace on the ground. The most plausible theory suggests that the stones were deliberately dragged by roller and sledge from the Preselis to the sea at Milford Haven. From there they were transported by rafts along the South Wales coast, then up the River Avon to a point near Frome in Somerset. From there the stones were probably pulled overland, and then floated down the River Wylye to Salisbury and up the Avon to West Amesbury, near Stonehenge.

In 2000, a Millennium Project attempted to re-enact this journey by moving a single 3-tonne Preseli bluestone block from its source to Stonehenge. Unfortunately, the design of their raft failed and the project was abandoned. The bluestone settings at Stonehenge are thought to have been re-arranged at least four times within a period of about 400 years between 2400 and 2000 BC.

Left: JMW Turner (1775-1851) painting of
Stonehenge during a storm

another World Heritage Site. There are various theories as to how the great inner and outer sarsen trilithons (two upright stones with a third as a lintel across the top), probably transported on log rollers from nearby Marlborough Downs, were erected. It has been calculated that it would have taken over 1,000 men seven weeks to transport just one large stone, and the total undertaking would have taken ten years – a remarkable feat of prehistoric organization and engineering.

Generally, it's now accepted that the smoothly dressed vertical stones, weighing about 26 tonnes each, were tipped into holes before being pulled upright. The lintels were raised on a gradually ascending platform of wooden scaffolding, and then carefully levered into place into lateral tongue-and-groove and vertical mortice-and-tenon joints. The builders even incorporated a curvature on both sides of the lintels to fit them within the diameter of the circle, described by Jacquetta Hawkes as 'an amazing refinement'.

Landscapes of Life – and Death

Our understanding of Stonehenge and its prehistoric ritual landscape has been totally transformed by the most recent theory among archaeologists. The six-year Stonehenge Riverside Project, begun in 2003 and funded by the Arts and Humanities Research Council, has concluded that Stonehenge was, in fact, an enormous cemetery during the third millennium BC – so far, evidence of 63 cremations has been unearthed.

The theory put forward by Professor Mike Parker Pearson of Sheffield University, who directed the project, is based on the grand stone monument being the domain of the ancestors, or the dead, and linked by a series of avenues and the River Avon to a domain of the living, represented by the neighbouring site of Durrington Walls. This was built of wood by the same people who created Stonehenge and at exactly the same time. Parker Pearson's hypothesis theory is that stone, a cold, inanimate substance, represents the dead, while the organic, living substance of wood is for the living. This symbolic commemoration of the dead may even be echoed in modern Christian funeral customs, which start with flowers at the graveside, followed by a simple wooden cross, finishing with the erection of a permanent gravestone. An enormous settlement site of around 1,000 houses, perhaps occupied by as many as 4,000 people, has also recently been identified at Durrington Walls, making it the largest Neolithic 'town' so far discovered in northern Europe. And evidence of feasting on a gargantuan scale, in the form of piles of discarded animal bones, seems to indicate it was an important gathering place during the winter solstice.

The nearby site of six concentric post holes, known as Woodhenge, is thought to have been a wooden building, predating Stonehenge and covered by a roof. In the 18th century, the ruler-straight, east–west embanked Cursus, a mile- (1.6km-) long

The so-called Amesbury Archer,
dubbed by the media as 'the King
of Stonehenge', was discovered in
2002 at Amesbury, a town 3 miles
(4.8km) from Stonehenge. The find
revealed that our forebears were
much more widely travelled than
had been previously suspected.
The grave of the strongly built,
35- to 45-year-old man, dating to
around 2300 BC, was the richest
early Bronze Age burial ever found
in Britain. And detailed forensic
tests carried out on the archer's
teeth and bones, and on the gold
hair tresses, copper knives, flint
arrowheads, wristguards and
pottery found in his grave, show
that he came from the region of
the Alps, perhaps modern-day
Switzerland. The copper knives
were from Spain and France. This
has been taken by archaeologists
as evidence of the wide trade
network that must have existed at
the time, and which first brought
metalworking to Britain. Judging
by the richness of the grave goods
buried with him, the archer was
obviously an important man, and
because he lived at the same time
as Stonehenge was first being
built, archaeologists have made
the intriguing prospect that he may
even have been involved in
its construction.

avenue about a mile (1.6km) north of Stonehenge, was taken to be a racecourse for the chariots of the Ancient Britons – a sort of Neolithic Epsom. Although this theory is no longer generally accepted, the original use of the Cursus still mystifies archaeologists, but the balance of opinion is that it must have held some kind of ceremonial importance to our Neolithic ancestors.

Avebury and associated sites

John Aubrey famously claimed that Avebury 'did as much excell Stoneheng (sic) as a Cathedral does a Parish Church'. Its great double circles were described by William Stukeley as '… that stupendous temple… the most august work at this day upon the globe of the earth'. He believed that Avebury and the linking prehistoric sites of Kennet and Beckhampton Avenues formed part of an enormous serpentine temple, which he named 'Dracontia', constructed by the Ancient Britons.

The great henge at Avebury, constructed some 4,500 years ago, encloses an area of nearly 30 acres within a huge ditch and bank, which was once 427m (1,400ft) wide and 9m (30ft) deep. Archaeologists have estimated that it would have taken an astonishing 1.5 million man hours to construct, using only the most primitive of tools such as deer-antler picks and shoulder-blade shovels. There can be no doubt that such a feat of engineering required an enormous amount of management and organization. The original 100 stones of the Great Circle at Avebury make it the largest stone circle in Europe, and it encloses much of the modern village. An important difference between the stones of Avebury and Stonehenge is that the former, the largest of which, the so-called Swindon Stone, weighs 65 tonnes, are not dressed like those at Stonehenge, but were erected just as they were found and transported from the Marlborough Downs. However, it's obvious that they were carefully selected for their shapes, with tall straight pillars alternating with broad diamond, or lozenge, shapes, which have been interpreted as male and female symbols.

Inside the Great Circle at Avebury, there are two other stone circles, known as the Northern and Southern Circles, which consisted originally of 27 and 29 stones respectively. The Northern Circle also had an internal concentric ring with 12 stones. The stones of Avebury were used as a convenient quarry by generations of local builders, and, in Puritan times, if they couldn't break them up, they would try to bury these prominent examples of the pagan past. The discovery of the skeleton of the barber-surgeon (see box, p.49) may be evidence of an unfortunate victim of such activity.

Overlooking Avebury and its associated avenues and sites is the Windmill Hill Causewayed Camp, which gave its name to the earliest Neolithic culture in Britain. Covering 21 acres and with a diameter of 360m (1,180ft), it is the largest such structure in the country, with three irregular concentric circles broken by a number of 'causeways'. It is thought that the camp served as a regional meeting place of local tribespeople, who may have also feasted and traded there.

The great, green, pudding-basin shape of nearby Silbury Hill – the largest man-made prehistoric mound in Europe – still manages to retain its secrets. Legend claims it is a monument to a King Sil, who is buried deep inside, decked out in gold and riding a golden horse. Despite several archaeological investigations, Silbury Hill's function remains a mystery, but it must have been important because it's been estimated that the 40-m (130-ft) high mound containing over 250,000 cubic metres of chalk must have taken 18 million man hours – or 500 workers at least ten years – to construct. Radiocarbon-dating from its core, where insects and seeds from the original ground level were found, has dated it to around 2145 BC.

Overlooking Silbury Hill across the busy A4 lies the wedge-shaped West Kennett Long Barrow, one of the largest and best-preserved Neolithic long barrows in the country, dated to around 3700 BC. It is over 1,000m (328ft) long and contains a passageway with four side chambers and an end chamber. The remains of 46 burials, from those of babies to old people, have been found inside these chambers. It is thought that the bones were deliberately disarticulated and may have been brought out regularly on ceremonial occasions. After being used for about 1,000 years, the tomb was filled in and the entrance blocked with a great (now restored) facade of upright sarsens.

Above: Aerial view of Avebury Stone Circle

As might be expected, the Stonehenge area has attracted its fair share of folklore. One of the most common myths refers to the healing qualities of the stones, first recorded by Geoffrey of Monmouth in his *History of the Kings of Britain* in the 12th century. He wrote: 'For in many of these stones is a mystery, and a healing virtue against many ailments...for they washed the stones and poured the water into baths, whereby those who were sick were cured. Moreover, they mixed confections of herbs with the water, whereby those who were wounded were healed, for not a stone is there that is wanting in virtue or leech-craft.'

The stones were apparently also useful as a pesticide, according to John Aubrey in the 17th century. He recounted: 'it is generally averred hereabouts that pieces (or powder) of these stones putt into their Wells doe drive away the Toades, with which their Wells are much infected, and this course they use still.'

But perhaps the most persistent folktale associates the stones of Stonehenge and Avebury, along with many other stone circles, with the Druids, a myth which was perpetuated by many later writers including men of letters such as Wordsworth, Blake and Dickens. Druidism in Britain is unlikely to date earlier than 400 BC, and its religious rites were performed in woodland groves and natural surroundings, never in built temples. The movement of those modern, latter-day Druids who congregate at Stonehenge for the summer solstice did not originate until the 19th century.

Left: Silbury Hill, the largest man-made mound in Europe
Above: Inside West Kennett Long Barrow

The South

Canterbury Cathedral, St Augustine's Abbey & St Martin's Church

It may be purely apocryphal, but the story of how Pope Gregory the Great came across some beautiful, fair-haired Anglo-Saxon children in Rome's slave market and remarked that they were not Angles but angels has endured for nearly 1,500 years. As a result of that chance encounter, in 597 Gregory reputedly sent Augustine and a group of monks to the coast of Kent as missionaries, to convert England to Christianity. The local king, Ethelbert, whose French queen Bertha was already a Christian, gifted the existing St Martin's Church at Canterbury – the building had been a place of worship during the Roman occupation – to Augustine to start his mission. On Christmas Day in the same year, over 10,000 of Ethelbert's subjects were baptized at what was referred to as the 'Miracle of Canterbury'.

From these humble beginnings, St Augustine established his seat (the Latin for seat is *cathedra*, from which cathedral is derived) within the Roman city walls of Canterbury (*Durovernum*) and built a Benedictine abbey and the first cathedral on the site of the present building. Ever since, there has been a Christian community in the city, making it the oldest in the English-speaking world. Together, Canterbury's magnificent Cathedral of Christ Church – the Mother Church of the Anglican

Above: Engraving showing the Baptism of King Ethelbert of Kent (c.552-616) by St Augustine at Canterbury in 597

Right: Canterbury Cathedral at sunset

'Will no one rid me of this turbulent priest?' Henry II's response to the actions of his former friend and ally Thomas Becket, whom he had appointed Archbishop of Canterbury in 1162, has echoed down through history. In June 1170, Roger de Pont l'Évêque, Archbishop of York, acting on instructions from the king, conducted the coronation of Henry's eldest son, also Henry, in York. Becket considered this a breach of Canterbury's privilege of coronation, and he excommunicated the offending archbishop. Word of this reached Henry on his sickbed in Normandy. His intemperate but probably innocent outburst was overheard by four knights who interpreted it as a royal command and set out immediately for Canterbury, arriving at the cathedral on 29 December 1170. Brandishing their naked swords, the four knights found Becket in the north transept, near the cloisters, where the monks were chanting vespers. The knights administered three mighty blows, the last one so violent that it sliced the top off his skull and shattered the blade's tip on the paved floor. Three days after his death, a series of miracles associated with Becket's martyrdom (now depicted in the windows of the Trinity Chapel) began. In 1173 he was canonized by Pope Alexander III.

Communion – the ruins of St Augustine's Abbey and St Martin's Church make up Canterbury's World Heritage Site, inscribed in 1987. According to UNESCO, the group of buildings reflected milestones in the history of Christianity in Britain, and successive architectural responses to Canterbury's developing role as the focus of the Church of England.

Canterbury Cathedral

Canterbury Cathedral is one of the largest, longest and most perfect examples of Early Gothic ecclesiastical architecture in Europe. The first stone-built cathedral was the work of the first Norman archbishop, Lanfranc (1070–1077). He rebuilt Augustine's ruined Saxon cathedral to a design based on the Abbey of St Etienne in Caen, where he had previously been abbot. The new cathedral was dedicated in 1077.

Following a disastrous fire in 1174, which destroyed the eastern end of the cathedral, the French architect William of Sens rebuilt the choir. An important example of Early English Gothic, it includes high pointed arches of dark Purbeck marble, flying buttresses and rib vaulting. Later, William the Englishman added the circular Corona Chapel and the Trinity Chapel at the eastern end, as a shrine for the relics of the martyr Thomas Becket, Archbishop of Canterbury (see box, left). The place where Becket's murder took place is still known as The Martyrdom. Other significant memorials in this part of the cathedral include the wonderful gleaming copper effigy of Edward Plantagenet (Edward III's son, aka the Black Prince), and the tombs of King Henry IV and his queen, Joan of Navarre. The magnificent 14th-century nave, 100m (328ft) long, was largely the work of master mason Henry Yevele, and is one of the best surviving examples of English Perpendicular Gothic. Taking 28 years to build, it replaced the much smaller Romanesque nave. Its soaring columns rise like a forest of stone to meet in delicate vaulted arches and beautiful gilt roof bosses. The entire cathedral is one of the longest in Europe, measuring 168m (550ft) from east to west.

The 11th-century Romanesque crypt is the oldest surviving part of the cathedral and the largest from that time anywhere in the country. Many details survive, including traces of contemporary wall painting in St Gabriel's Chapel and an array of carved capitals and decorated columns.

The superb multi-pinnacled late Perpendicular Central, or Bell Harry Tower, was built in 1496 to house a bell previously donated by Henry of Eastry, Prior of Christ Church, Canterbury. The original Norman northwest tower was demolished in the late 1700s due to structural problems. It was replaced during the 1830s with a Perpendicular-style copy of the southwest tower. Known as the Arundel Tower, it gives a welcome and satisfying symmetry to the western end of the cathedral.

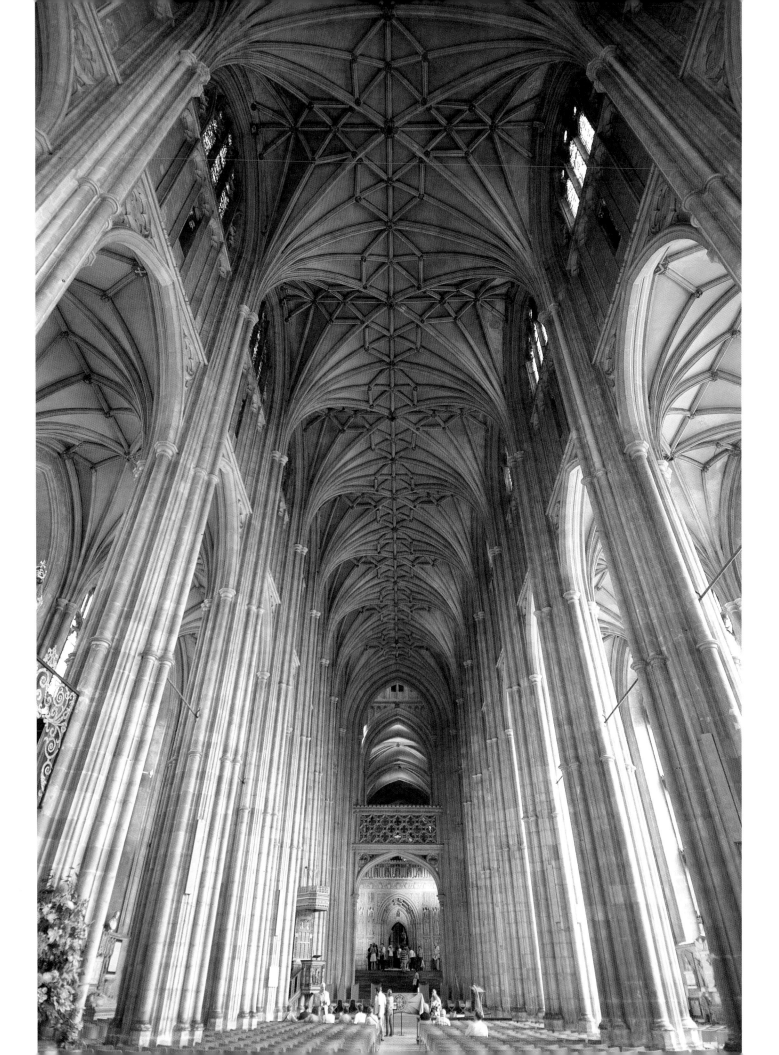

The cathedral is set within its own walled Precincts, surrounded by medieval buildings and ruins. These include the Water Tower, a Romanesque gem that was once the source of the monastic water supply, and the monastery's granary, bakery and brewery, now part of King's School. The Chapter House, with its lofty oak roof and raised seat for the prior, is the largest of its kind in England.

Standing to the east of the cathedral are the substantial and still impressive foundations of St Augustine's Abbey, managed by English Heritage. The abbey was founded as a Benedictine monastery and burial place for the Anglo-Saxon kings of Kent by Augustine in 597, the same year he arrived in Kent. The great crenellated gate from 1309 leads into the ruins – their damage in an earthquake in 1538 was merely a foretaste of what was to come during Henry VIII's Dissolution of the Monasteries later that year. The abbey's wonderful library of over 2,000 books, many of which were probably produced in the abbey's own scriptorium, were also destroyed during the Dissolution.

St Martin's Church, the simple building in which Augustine and his followers first worshipped, also stands to the east of the cathedral, outside the city walls. It is believed to be the oldest functioning place of worship in England today. It includes some Roman brickwork dating from the 4th century, and the font, made from Caen stone, is richly decorated with rows of intersecting arches and circles.

Left: Inside Canterbury Cathedral
Above: Stained glass depiction of St Augustine
Above right: The ruins of St Augustine's Abbey

Maritime Greenwich

The Thames at Greenwich has played such an important and pivotal role in England's history that it prompted Thames-lover John Burns, Liberal MP for Battersea and former President of the Board of Trade, to compare it with other great waterways of the world. In 1929, he famously remarked, 'The Saint Lawrence is water, the Mississippi is muddy water, but the Thames is liquid history.'

The position of Greenwich, commanding the main land and water routes from Continental Europe to the capital, has made it a key strategic site since Roman times. But it was during the Jacobean and Stuart periods that Greenwich was transformed to become one of the finest cultural landscapes in Britain, a centre for classical architecture, naval endeavour and the pursuit of the sciences.

Maritime Greenwich was inscribed as a World Heritage Site in 1997. This was in recognition of its unique collection of classical buildings within the Royal Park on the eastern edge of London, which bear witness to the period of unparalleled artistic, scientific and navel endeavour during the 17th and 18th centuries.

The royal connection

Greenwich has had royal connections for over six centuries. The royal park, the first of its kind, was enclosed for hunting in the 15th century. Placentia, the royal palace facing the Thames at Greenwich, was a favourite residence of Henry VII. It was here, as Dr Johnson recorded, that both Henry VIII and Elizabeth I were born. When Henry came to the throne in 1509, he built stables, rebuilt the chapel and added a tiltyard with towers and a viewing gallery, so that visitors could admire him performing his favourite martial displays, including jousting.

Although Elizabeth spent most of her summers at Greenwich, she did little new building there. She dined on board Francis Drake's *Golden Hind* at nearby Deptford following his successful circumnavigation of the world in 1580, and knighted him soon afterwards. And legend has it that the old Deptford to Woolwich road, over which The Queen's House was later built, was where Sir Walter Raleigh laid down his cloak so that Elizabeth would not step into a puddle. When Elizabeth's distant relative James I succeeded her in 1603, he built new lodgings in Greenwich Park for his wife, Anne of Denmark. Shortly afterwards, he assigned the entire palace to her, and in 1616 she employed the celebrated architect Inigo Jones to design and start building what is still known as The Queen's House, perhaps the first purely classical Renaissance building in the country. After Anne died in 1619, the work was completed by Queen Henrietta Maria, wife of Charles I, in 1629. An outstanding feature is the beautiful Tulip Stairs, the first centrally unsupported spiral staircase in Britain, completed in about 1635 and named after the repeated tulip pattern in the wrought-iron balustrade.

It was not until the triumphant restoration of Charles II in 1660 after the bitter and divisive Civil War that royal attention could be turned back to the palace of Greenwich. Charles determined to replace it with a contemporary modern structure of three ranges, open to the mighty Thames. His master plan was to be executed by John Webb, a pupil of Inigo Jones, and work started on the first domed block, known as King Charles Court in 1664. It was not completed, however, until Mary II, wife and joint ruler with William II, turned her attention to Greenwich. The matching Queen Mary Court did not follow until 1751.

Mary determined that Charles II's single range of buildings should be 'converted and employed as a hospital for seamen', and that the adjoining area, still occupied by the decaying Tudor palace of Henry and Elizabeth, should be used to extend it to fulfil Charles's original plan of 30 years before.

Above: Painting by Canaletto of Greenwich Hospital from
the north bank of the Thames
Overleaf: Greenwich Park and Royal Observatory

The completion of the iconic group of buildings as seen from the river, now known collectively as the Old Royal Naval College, was begun in 1696. The designs were by Sir Christopher Wren, who had remodelled much of London upriver after the Great Fire of 1666, and Nicholas Hawksmoor. Originally called the Royal Hospital for Seamen, a role it fulfilled until 1869, this fine grouping of monumental classical architecture is now home to the University of Greenwich and the Trinity College of Music.

Alongside the riches of its exterior design, perfectly captured soon after its completion in Canaletto's famous view from the Thames of 1751, some of the College's interiors are equally stunning. They include James Thornhill's allegorical baroque masterpiece of the painted ceiling and walls of *The Painted Hall* (for which he was paid £3 per square yard for the ceiling and £1 for the walls), and James 'Athenian' Stuart and William Newton's magnificent neoclassical Chapel, with its nautical cable-patterned marble floor and Benjamin West's painted altarpiece of St Paul's shipwreck on Malta.

Discover Greenwich is a new £6m cultural venue at the Old Royal Naval College, which opened in March 2010. The Lottery-funded centre interprets the history of Maritime Greenwich for up to a million visitors a year, and is the starting point for understanding and appreciating the World Heritage Site. The new centre includes an exhibition hall, the Clore Learning Centre and a temporary exhibition gallery. There's also a shop, a tourist information centre, and, in the adjacent former brewery, a cafe, brasserie and bar, with its own exhibition charting the history of brewing in London and Greenwich.

Charles II was also a great supporter of the sciences. He appointed John Flamsteed of Derby as the first Astronomer Royal in 1675, charging him 'to apply himself with the most exact care and diligence to rectifying the tables of the motions of the heavens, and the places of the fixed stars, so as to find out the so much desired longitude of places for the perfecting of the art of navigation' (see box, right).

The Royal Observatory, on top of the hill in Greenwich Park, is centred on Flamsteed House, the original observatory. It was designed in 1675 by Sir Christopher Wren for, as he put it, 'the Observator's habitation… and a little for pompe'. The building's romantic, almost fairy-tale castle appearance belies its purpose as the first specifically scientific research establishment in Britain. The orange Time Ball, which tops one of the pinnacles, drops every day at precisely 1pm, and was originally used by ships passing along the Thames to set their chronometers. Inside is The Octagon Room, little changed from Francis Place's engraving of 1676, where important visitors could observe the long telescopes in use. The room is still watched over by portraits of Charles II and James II. It was, nevertheless, in the shed-like Observatory – later, the

SOLVING THE PROBLEM OF LONGITUDE

An unheard-of Lincolnshire clockmaker, John Harrison of Barrow-on-Humber, cracked what was called the greatest scientific problem of the mid-18th century – how mariners should measure longitude. Latitude – their north–south position – could be ascertained by measuring the angle between the horizon and the sun at its meridian at noon. But longitude – the east–west position – depended on having an accurate timepiece to find another fixed, or 'prime', meridian, and to calculate accurately the time difference between the two. The problem was solved by John Harrison's 'chronometer', which he invented in 1759. In this accurate, seaworthy timepiece, the problem of a rolling deck was solved by a high-precision, friction-free mechanism. It put longitudinal calculations within reach of most seamen, and it was used by Captain James Cook on his Pacific voyage of 1772–75. The Longitude Act of 1714 offered a reward of £20,000 – an astonishing sum, worth about £1.5 million today – for a method to determine longitude to an accuracy of half a degree. Harrison travelled to London to present his 34-kg (75-lb) H1 chronometer to the Board of Longitude in June 1737, confident that he would win the prize. The clock is still kept at The Royal Observatory, where it is wound every day and keeps good time.

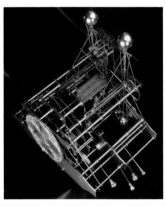

Quadrant House – where Flamsteed established the first Greenwich Meridian. The meridian line was then moved east to the present Meridian Building and then to the Great Equatorial Building, with its onion-shaped dome.

Zero degrees longitude, the prime meridian of the world since 1884, is marked by a brass-edged plate glass line across the paved courtyard of the Old Royal Observatory. It is, quite literally, the place where East meets West. The line is 'splitting the globe in two equal halves with all the authority of the Equator', as Dava Sobel describes it in her 1995 best-seller *Longitude*. This is where the world sets its watch, and you can buy a souvenir ticket to mark the exact time when you straddled the meridian. At night, a bright green laser beam projects the meridian 10 miles (16km) north across the Thames and towards distant Epping Forest in Essex.

Larger than the Old Royal Observatory, the South Observatory was completed in 1899. After refurbishment, it re-opened to the public in 2007 as an astronomy centre, which includes the striking truncated bronze cone of the 120-seat Peter Harrison Planetarium. The building is named after its major benefactor, the computer services magnate Peter Harrison. It should be pointed out that he is unrelated to John Harrison (see box, left), the man who invented the chronometer, which first made the calculation of longitude possible.

Situated to the west of the Queen's House, the National Maritime Museum, which includes the Queen's House and the Royal Observatory, is the largest of its kind in the world. The estimated two million items in the museum include 4,000 maritime paintings, 70,000 prints and drawings, 2,500 models, 100,000 books and a million photographs, many of which are on display.

For the visitor, the most striking architectural feature of the museum is probably Neptune Court. Built in 1997, this vast, well-lit atrium beneath a glass and steel roof spans the area between the 19th-century west wings of the museum. It replaced the 19th-century Neptune's Hall. The top-lit rotunda in the west wing was inserted by Sir Edwin Lutyens in the 1930s.

The 183-acre Greenwich Park is the oldest of the royal parks. It was established by Humphrey, Duke of Gloucester and regent to his nephew, the young Henry VI, in 1433, when he enclosed heathland, woodland and pasture within a wooden fence for hunting purposes. James I replaced the fence around the park with a 3.5-m (12-ft) high, 2-mile (3.2-km) long brick wall in the early 17th century. A small herd of fallow and red deer still lives in the park.

THE *CUTTY SARK*

Originally built in 1869 in Dumbarton and designed to last only 30 years, the stately 963-tonne clipper was used in the high-value tea trade to India. But the same year that the *Cutty Sark* was built saw the opening of the Suez Canal, which effectively spelt the end of the tea-clipper trade. She was transferred to the Australian wool run, and it was under the command of Captain Richard Woodget between 1885–95 that she really made her name. On Woodget's first voyage in 1885, she defeated her old tea-trade rival *Thermopylae* on a voyage from Sydney by over a week, arriving back in Britain after only 73 days at sea.

After a period under the Portuguese flag as the Ferreira from 1895, the *Cutty Sark* was used as a training ship by the Thames Nautical College at Greenhithe in 1938, and eventually came to rest at Greenwich in 1954, after 'starring' at the Festival of Britain.

And her name? It comes from Robert Burns's poem 'Tam O'Shanter' and refers to the short shift ('cutty sark') worn by the witch Nannie, whose white-painted figure features as the ship's figurehead. Nearby is the white-hulled *Gipsy Moth* IV, the 16-m (54-ft) ketch in which Sir Francis Chichester sailed around the world in 226 days in 1967.

The park was remodelled by Charles II, and a surviving plan by André le Nôtre, creator of the park at Versailles, shows that he wanted to create a formal parterre with raised side avenues centred on the Queen's House. The plan was only partly executed, although many of the avenues of chestnut trees and the Giant Steps, or terraces, which link the lower and upper parts of the park, still survive.

Greenwich Park has been open to the public since 1705, although this was not on a regular basis until the 1830s. Then it became notorious for 'improper' holiday behaviour, such as young ladies tumbling down the hill in various stages of undress. Dickens likened this to the breaking out of 'a spring rash: a three day's fever, which cools the blood for six months afterwards.'

Perhaps the finest thing about Greenwich Park is its outstanding views across London from the summit of the hill. They take in the giant meander of the Thames around the Isle of Dogs, the former hub of the British Empire's maritime trade and now more familiar to viewers in the titles of the popular BBC TV soap opera EastEnders.

Looking west on a clear day, you can make out the dome of Christopher Wren's best-known masterpiece, St Paul's Cathedral, in the heart of the city. Meanwhile, the view to the north is dominated by Richard Rogers' gigantic Millennium Dome, now the O2, a 20,000-seat sporting and concert arena. To the east lies the modern business centre of Docklands, watched over by the 50-storey Canary Wharf Tower, the highest building in Britain at 235m (770ft).

Above: Inside Greenwich's St Peter & St Paul Chapel
Right: The spiral staircase in the Queen's House, Greenwich

Royal Botanic Gardens, Kew

When Augusta, widow of Frederick, Prince of Wales, set about enlarging and extending the gardens at Kew in 1759, her ambition was to create a garden that would 'contain all the plants known on Earth'. Two hundred and fifty years later, Augusta's dream is a step closer to reality, with the creation in 2000 of the Millennium Seed Bank at Wakehurst Place, the Sussex satellite of the Royal Botanic Gardens. This now stores seeds from virtually the whole (96 per cent) of Britain's flora, and 10 per cent of the entire world's flora.

The Royal Botanic Gardens, usually known as Kew Gardens, covers 300 acres of gardens, glasshouses and grasslands between Richmond and Kew on the outskirts of southwest London. It is an internationally important botanical research and education institution, employing about 700 people and attracting about two million visitors every year. Kew Gardens celebrated its 250th anniversary in 2009.

The collections at Kew already constitute the world's largest collection of living plants. Over 40,000 are held there, and the herbarium, which is also the largest in the world, has over seven million preserved plant specimens. The Kew site also includes four Grade I and 36 Grade II listed buildings in an internationally significant landscape. Kew Gardens was created a World Heritage Site in 2003, fulfilling UNESCO's criteria for 'the interchange of values, as a testimony to the cultural tradition, and in their significance to human history'. The gardens have made a significant contribution to the international study of plant diversity and to economic botany, and are notable as much for the richness of their collections of plants as for their landscaping and architectural features. Important figures in their creation include Charles Bridgeman, William Kent and 'Capability' Brown.

History of the gardens

The ultra-modern glasshouses and other buildings that now greet visitors to Kew are a far cry from their humble beginnings in the 18th century. Augusta's plots were developed from Lord Henry Capel's 17th-century garden at Kew Farm, famous for its apples, and eventually became part of the neighbouring royal estates of Kew and Richmond. Augusta's husband Frederick wasn't much liked by his father George II, who denounced him as 'a monster and the greatest villian that ever was born'. By the time George succeeded to the throne in 1727, Frederick and Augusta had moved to

Kew Farm, covering the house with white stucco and renaming it the White House. While Queen Caroline, Frederick's mother, employed Charles Bridgeman to landscape the Richmond estate (much to the disgust of her grumpy husband George II, who regarded his wife's gardening activities as 'childish, silly stuff'), Frederick and Augusta created a great lawn, kitchen garden, lake and melon ground at Kew with the assistance of their friend Lord Bute, a skilled gardener. When Frederick died suddenly in 1751, Augusta continued to develop Kew to create her vision of a comprehensive global Garden of Eden. Unknowingly, she planted the seeds for today's Royal Botanic Gardens.

George III, Frederick and Augusta's son, further enhanced the gardens, aided by William Aiton and, notably, Sir Joseph Banks (see box, left). Frederick and Augusta's White House was demolished in 1802. The adjoining Dutch House, the plain brick structure built by the Dutch merchant Samuel Fortrey in 1631 on the banks of the Thames, is now known as Kew Palace. It was purchased by George III in 1781 as a nursery for his children, and remains the smallest and most intimate of all the royal palaces. The plant collection grew haphazardly until the appointment of the first official collector, Francis Masson, in 1771. In 1840, the gardens were adopted as a national botanical garden. Sir William Hooker, who was appointed Kew's first official Director a year later, worked tirelessly to increase the size of the gardens. By 1904, they had reached their present size of 300 acres.

In the 19th century, the first successful attempt at propagating rubber trees outside South America took place at Kew. Less auspiciously, in February 1913, the Tea House was burnt down by suffragettes Olive Wharry and Lilian Lenton. The most recent catastrophe to affect Kew was the Great Storm of October 1987, when hundreds of trees were lost.

Highlights of the gardens

The architect Sir William Chambers designed several buildings for Augusta, but perhaps the most famous surviving example is the 10-storey, 50-m (163-ft) high Chinese Pagoda, in the southeastern corner of the gardens. Built in 1762 at the height of the craze for all things Chinese, it is claimed that the 80 glass dragons that once adorned the folly were removed to help pay George IV's debts.

Kew's most iconic feature is probably the Palm House, designed by architect Decimus Burton to echo his Great Conservatory at Chatsworth in Derbyshire, and built between 1844 and 1848. Ironfounder Richard Turner persuaded Burton that he could do away with central supporting struts by using wrought iron to span the large widths in the building. It was a technique borrowed from the shipbuilding industry and, from a distance, the glasshouse can resemble the upturned hull of a boat.

Left: Cheeky statue in the Queen's Garden at Kew Gardens
Overleaf: The Palm House Pond with fountain depicting Hercules wrestling river god Achelous, Kew Gardens

The light, lofty space inside was designed to accommodate the crowns of large palms, which were then being collected and introduced to Europe. Heating was obviously important for the care of these tender plants, so boilers were placed in the basement, which sent heat into the glasshouse via water pipes running beneath iron gratings in the floor. A 150-m (490-ft) long tunnel ran between the Palm House and the Italianate campanile smoke stack, which still stands beside Victoria Gate. It served the dual purpose of carrying away fumes and bringing coal to the boilers by underground railway. The Palm House is now heated by gas. Today, the tallest palms are located beneath the lofty central dome. These include the peach palm (*Bactris gasipaes*), babassu palm (*Attalea speciosa*), queen palm (*Syagrus romanzoffiana*) and the coconut palm (*Cocos nucifera*).

Burton was also responsible for the smaller Waterlily House near by, which was completed in 1852. It was built to contain the enormous plate-like leaves of the Amazonian waterlily, *Victoria amazonica*, which can grow to over 2.5m (8ft) in diameter. A mature leaf can support a child, or over 45kg (7 stone) in weight, provided the load is evenly distributed. But the plant never thrived here and, today, a close relative, *Victoria cruziana*, inhabits the enclosed pond.

The Temperate House, which is twice as large as the Palm House, followed later in the 19th century. It is the largest Victorian glasshouse in the world, 19m (63ft) high and covering an area of 4,880sq m (5,850sq yd). Sir William Hooker commissioned Burton to design the Temperate House in 1859, and it was officially opened, still unfinished, in 1863. Soaring costs meant that it would not be completed for another 40 years. Today, the South Wing and Octagon are home to African plants; the main rectangular hall hosts subtropical trees and palms; while the North Wing and Octagon contain temperate plants from Australia, New Zealand, Asia and the Pacific, some of which were first brought to Kew by Sir Joseph Banks (see box, p.73). A boiler helps keep the temperature at a minimum 18°C (64°F) all year round, and the sun provides a little extra warmth for the heat-loving tropical plants at the southern end.

The northeastern corner of the gardens is dominated by the striking modernistic glass gables of the Princess of Wales Conservatory, named in honour of Augusta, the founder of the gardens, and opened by her successor, Princess Diana, in 1987. This is the most complex of Kew's public glasshouses, with ten computer-controlled climatic zones under one roof.

Most of the conservatory is taken up with the dry and wet tropics zones, but there are eight other different microclimates, each created for the special needs of a particular plant group. All plants are shown as naturally as possible, with ferns clinging to dripping rock faces, and climbers wriggling up columns.

Above: Spiral stairs take visitors into the leafy roof space of the Palm House
Top right: William Chambers' Chinese Pagoda

Paths on different levels bring visitors as close as possible to the plants, so they can appreciate the details.

The Syon Vista on the western side of the gardens looks out across the River Thames towards 18th-century Syon House on the opposite bank. Designed by Robert Adam, this London home of the Duke of Northumberland stands in a 200-acre 'Capability' Brown landscaped park. Nearby is Kew's main Lake, which lies east–west across the western side of the gardens, and was created in 1856 by Sir William Hooker from an area excavated to provide gravel for terracing the new Temperate House. The surplus gravel was used to build the four islands.

The Lake is crossed by the sinuous lines of the Sackler Crossing, named after Dr Mortimer and Theresa Sackler, whose donation paid for its creation. It was designed by the architect John Pawson and opened in 2006. The sweeping black granite walkway carries visitors low over the water along a curving path, mimicking the lake's rounded banks. The bridge forms part of a new route around the gardens, designed to give access to less frequented areas. It takes visitors from the Temperate House and Evolution House – a gift from the Australian Government in 1949, used initially to display Australian flora but now leads visitors on a 3.5-billion-year-journey through Earth's history – to the lake and then on towards the Japanese Minka House, Bamboo Garden and the Brentford Gate.

The Tower of London

Legend claims that should the Tower of London's famous ravens (*Corvus corax*) leave, both the Tower and the monarchy will crumble. There have been ravens at the Tower at least since the time of Charles II.

At least ten ravens (six on duty and four spare youngsters) are kept at the Tower, housed next to the Wakefield Tower. The Ravenmaster, a member of the Yeomen Warders (see box, p.80), is responsible for their welfare. He hand-rears fledglings over a period of about six weeks before they are ready for duty.

The ravens live an average of 25 years, but some have been known to reach the age of 45. They are fed on raw meat, which is brought daily from Smithfield Meat Market by the Ravenmaster. Apparently, this daily ration is behind the Yeomen Warders' comment that the only real beefeaters at the Tower of London are the ravens.

One wing of every raven is clipped by the Ravenmaster to unbalance their flight and prevent them from flying away. The birds are, however, free to roam the grounds, but visitors are advised not to feed them because they have been known to inflict a vicious peck.

Somehow the sinister croaking of the Tower of London's famous glossy, black-feathered ravens (see box, left) echoing around Tower Green seems to be perfectly in keeping with the dark deeds that have been committed here. At least seven members of the aristocracy, including Henry VIII's second and fifth wives, Anne Boleyn (1536) and Catherine Howard (1542), plus the tragic 'Queen for Nine Days', Lady Jane Grey (1554), and Elizabeth I's former favourite Robert Devereux, the 2nd Earl of Essex (1601), were executed for treason here, by the swing of the executioner's axe. George, Duke of Clarence, the brother of Edward IV, was also executed for treason in the Tower in February 1478. When Edward died, his two young sons became the famous Princes in the Tower, who were allegedly murdered on the orders of his other brother Richard, Duke of Gloucester, later Richard III. The last execution to take place at the Tower, by a firing squad formed by the Scots Guards, was that of the German spy Josef Jakobs in August 1941.

Being 'sent to the Tower' has always been the equivalent of a death sentence in Britain, and the threatening presence of the White Tower and its associated battlements – one

THE FIRST LONDON ZOO

A royal menagerie was first established in the Tower in the early 13th century, possibly during the reign of King John. It was probably stocked with lions, leopards, lynxes and camels, from an earlier menagerie started in 1125 by Henry I at his palace, later Blenheim, in Woodstock, near Oxford (see p.90).

There was certainly a menagerie at the Tower in 1235, when Henry III received a wedding gift of three leopards from the Holy Roman Emperor, Frederick II. A polar bear, a gift from the king of Norway, was added to the collection in 1252, and in 1264 the animals were moved to the Bulwark Tower, later renamed the Lion Tower. A lion skull found there has been radiocarbon-dated to between 1280 and 1385, making it the earliest medieval big cat known in Britain. The menagerie was occasionally opened to the public during the reign of Elizabeth I.

Animal welfare and commercial reasons eventually led to the animals being moved to London Zoo when it opened in Regent's Park in 1828. The last of the animals actually left in 1835, and most of the Lion Tower was demolished soon afterwards, although Lion Gate remains.

of the most complete medieval military complexes in the country – has dominated the London skyline for well over nine centuries. It was inscribed as a World Heritage Site in 1988.

A brief tour of the Tower

The dominating, four-square shape of the 27-m (90-ft) high White Tower was built by William the Conqueror in 1078 to the design of Gundulf, Bishop of Rochester, inside London's city walls and adjacent to the Thames. In those troubled times, it was built as much to protect the Normans from the citizens of London as to protect London from outside invaders. Gundulf used white limestone imported from Caen, France for the quoins and windows, but the massive walls, tapering from 4.5-m (15-ft) to 3.3-m (11-ft) thick, were built from local Kentish ragstone. Rising above the battlements are four turrets, three of which are square and one circular, in order to accommodate the spiral staircase. This turret was briefly used as the first Royal Observatory (see p.68) during the reign of Charles II. Completing the original defences to the south of the White Tower was the enclosed bailey. In the 1190s, Richard I enclosed the White Tower within a curtain wall, and had a moat dug around it, filled with water from the Thames. To the east, Richard utilized the existing Roman city wall as part of the circuit. Part of this was incorporated into the later curtain wall of Henry III and still exists today, running between the Bloody Tower and the Bell Tower. The White Tower gets its name from the fact that, in 1240, Henry III had the exterior of the building whitewashed to make it look even more formidable. The only original part remaining of the White Tower's interior on the first floor is the evocative St John's Chapel, one of the most complete surviving examples of early Anglo-Norman ecclesiastical architecture. Resembling the choir of a Romanesque church with its apse and ambulatory, the chapel is one of the architectual highlights of the Tower.

Above left: *The Execution of Lady Jane Grey,* painted in 1833 by Delaroche
Right: Traitor's Gate, Tower of London

Henry III transformed the Tower into a major royal residence in the early 13th century, incorporating palatial buildings within the Inner Bailey to the south of the White Tower. Henry also built a massive 13-towered outer curtain wall from 1238 onwards. The Wakefield Tower, the largest of the new curtain wall towers, where, legend has it, the imprisoned Henry VI was murdered in 1471, and the Lanthorn Tower were integral parts of this new royal palace, adjoining the now demolished Great Hall. The Tower remained a royal residence until the time of Oliver Cromwell, who demolished many of Henry's palatial buildings.

Other towers in the curtain wall include the Martin Tower, where the Crown Jewels were kept from 1669 until 1842; the Bell Tower, which is the oldest tower, built in the 1190s and named after the curfew bell that has been rung from here for over 500 years, and incorporated into Henry III's modifications; and the Bloody (or Garden) Tower, which takes its grisly name from the legend that the Princes in the Tower were murdered there. Between 1275 and 1285, Edward I built an additional outer curtain wall, completely enclosing the inner walls and creating a concentric defence. He filled in the old moat and built a new one. This outer curtain wall has five towers facing the Thames, including the river entrance to the Tower beneath St Thomas's Tower. The entrance is known as Traitors' Gate because prisoners accused of treason, such as Anne Boleyn and Sir Thomas More, are believed to have passed through it.

The Crown Jewels have been kept at the Tower of London since 1303. After the coronation of Charles II, they were locked away and shown only on payment of a fee, but this arrangement ended when Col Thomas Blood stole the jewels in 1671. The Crown Jewels are now kept in secure conditions in the Jewel House, which opened in 1994. Here, visitors can still admire the magnificent, jewel-encrusted Imperial State Crown, used at coronations and at the State Opening of Parliament.

The Royal Armouries, now housed over three floors of the White Tower, date from the Middle Ages, when armour was made here for royalty. By the time of Charles II, there was a permanent public display, making it among the first museums in Britain. In 1414, the Tower became home to the Master of the Ordnance and the Ordnance Office (later the Board of Ordnance), which was responsible for providing weapons to the Armed Forces. The Board of Ordnance was abolished in 1855, but only a small part of the historic collection could ever be displayed due to space restrictions. So, in 1995, much of the artillery collection was moved to Fort Nelson in Hampshire, and the following year the new Royal Armouries Museum was opened in Leeds. However, the White Tower still holds an important collection of arms and armour dating from the Middle Ages, notably that belonging to the Tudor and Stuart kings, in particular Henry VIII.

Right: The White Tower, seen across the River Thames

ENTRY TO THE TRAITORS' GATE

Westminster Palace & Abbey

The present Palace of Westminster, better known as the Houses of Parliament, is such an integral part of the modern London scene that it's hard to believe it has existed for less than 150 years. Its inscription, along with the adjacent medieval Westminster Abbey and St Margaret's Church, the parish church of Parliament, as a World Heritage Site in 1987 confirmed its position as the keystone of England's history, and the birthplace of the Mother of Parliaments.

There has been a royal palace at Westminster since the 11th century. It was originally built by Edward the Confessor, who also re-endowed a Benedictine monastery on Thorney Island (see box, p.86) in the Thames and erected the first stone-built church dedicated to St Peter (see box, right) on the site of the Abbey. The only remnant of Edward's abbey is in the round, sprung arches of the Undercroft, now used as the Abbey Museum.

The Palace of Westminster

The present Palace of Westminster, correctly known as the New Palace, is the result of a competition for designing a new building after the old one, the principal residence of English monarchs from Edward the Confessor to Henry VIII, went up in flames in October 1843. The only remains of the old palace are the Jewel Tower and the magnificent Westminster Hall. Originally built by William Rufus, son of William the Conqueror, between 1097 and 1099, the Hall was the venue for the first elected parliament called by Simon de Montfort in 1265.

It was perhaps appropriate that the competition was won by Charles Barry, who was born in nearby Bridge Street, Westminster, in 1795. His magnificent design for an unrestrained, Perpendicular Gothic-style building took over 30 years to complete and contains over 1,100 rooms organized around two ranks of courtyards, 126 staircases and more than 3 miles (4.8km) of corridors. It covers 8 acres, with its main facade extending over 265m (872ft) along the river front. At the time, the Palace of Westminster was the largest building in Britain. Barry was assisted by a man he described as 'his comet', Augustus Pugin, a leading authority on Gothic architecture and style, who provided the designs for the lavish interior decoration and furnishings.

The 96m (315ft) Clock Tower at the northeastern end of the Palace has become a much-loved landmark. Affectionately known as Big Ben – strictly speaking the name refers only to the 13-tonne main bell that strikes the hours – the tower is one of three that dominate the pinnacles and turrets of the Palace. The others are the 100m (336ft) Victoria Tower, which features the sovereign's entrance at its base, and the lower spire of the Central Tower, built to improve ventilation.

The main business of the Palace is, of course, providing a home for the House of Commons and the House of Lords, the two-tier system that governs the country and which became the model for many other administrations all over the world. The House of Lords is perhaps the crowning glory of Pugin's Gothic exuberance, and is the scene of the annual State Opening of Parliament. The House of Commons is slightly more restrained in appearance, but this is where the political power of the country is centred. Between the two is the hub of the building, the magnificent vaulted octagon of the Central Lobby, lined with statues of 19th-century statesmen, where people come to 'lobby' their MPs.

Westminster Abbey

The Westminster Abbey we see today is largely the work of Henry III. He was determined to honour his great hero Edward the Confessor, and had been inspired by the French cathedrals at Amiens and Chartres. Henry ordered 'a magnificent

THE LEGEND OF ST PETER'S CATCH

On the night before the dedication of the original minster at Westminster in the 7th century, a lone traveller appeared to a fisherman on the south bank of the Thames, asking him for safe passage across the river.

After crossing the river, the traveller entered the new church, which had been built by Mellitus, Bishop of London on the orders of Sebert, a Saxon king of Essex. As he did so, a brilliant, heavenly light engulfed the building, and the air was filled with the song of angels and the heavenly host. The fisherman watched dazzled and terrified by what he had seen.

When the traveller left the church, he asked the fisherman if he had anything to eat. On replying that he had caught nothing, the stranger told the fisherman to let down his nets as they recrossed the river. When the fisherman did so, he found them miraculously bulging with salmon. The traveller told the awestruck fisherman to take the biggest fish to Bishop Mellitus as a gift, and identified himself as St Peter, to whom the new church was to be dedicated.

Left: Floodlit Houses of Parliament viewed from the South Bank
Overleaf: Stained glass window of the Battle of Britain, Westminster Abbey

WESTMINSTER PALACE & ABBEY   83

DOWDING   HAR

PORTAL

shrine to be made out of purest refined gold and precious stones, to be constructed in London by the most skilled goldsmiths, for the deposition of the relics of the blessed Edward'. Work began on his Gothic masterpiece in 1245. His work can still be seen today – in the Nave, at 31m (102ft), the highest in England; the Quire; North and South Transepts; the Chapter House; and Sacrarium, where the shrine to St Edward the Confessor still dominates, and where the coronations of 38 kings and queens of England have been carried out.

The venerable oak, graffiti-covered Coronation Chair, kept in St Edward's Chapel, was built on the orders of Henry's son Edward I, early in the 14th century. It formerly contained the Stone of Scone or Stone of Destiny, which was returned to Edinburgh Castle in 1996 (see box, p.175).

Generations of the great and good from all walks of British life have memorials in the Abbey, notably 28 kings and queens, and a host of poets and writers, including Shakespeare, Chaucer, Charles Dickens (for whom celebrations honouring the bicentenary of his birth are planned here in 2012) and T.S. Eliot in the clutter of Poet's Corner in the South Transept. But perhaps the most moving memorials are those to the Unknown Warrior in the Nave, representing the unnamed dead of World War I, which was dedicated on Armistice Day in 1920; and the simple, circular memorial to the Innocent Victims of Oppression, Violence and War outside the west front of the Abbey, which was dedicated in 1996.

Above: Westminster Hall in the Palace of Westminster
Right: Ornate splendour at Westminster Abbey

The Midlands

Blenheim Palace

Derwent Valley Mills

Ironbridge Gorge

Blenheim Palace

As we passed through the entrance archway and the lovely scenery burst upon me, Randolph said with pardonable pride, 'This is the finest view in England.' Looking at the lake, the bridge, the miles of magnificent park studded with old oaks… and the huge and stately palace, I confess I felt awed. But my American pride forbade the admission.

This 'awesome' initial view of Blenheim Palace, just outside Woodstock in Oxfordshire, was experienced by Jennie Jerome, daughter of the American stockbroker millionaire Leonard Jerome, and wife of Lord Randolph Churchill, son of the 7th Duke of Marlborough. On their marriage in 1874, she became known as Lady Randolph Churchill. The couple's first son, Winston, the future wartime Prime Minister, was born in that 'huge and stately palace' in the same year (see box, right). Visitors to the palace, which became a World Heritage Site in 1986 and was once described as 'the English Versailles', can see the small room where he was born, to the right of the Great Hall.

A tour of the palace

Blenheim Palace, a masterpiece of English baroque architecture, was a gift from the nation in 1704 to John Churchill, 1st Duke of Marlborough, in grateful recognition of his victories over the French, most notably at Blenheim (more correctly, Blindheim in Bavaria), during the War of the Spanish Succession. The gift consisted of the medieval Royal Manor of Woodstock, where Elizabeth I had been imprisoned for her alleged part in the Wyatt Plot in 1554, and the sum of £240,000 for the construction of the palace.

Although Blenheim was never actually Winston Churchill's home, his love of the place remained throughout his long life, and it was always where he felt his roots to be. The estate and family title had passed to his cousin, the 9th Duke but, for five years during the 1890s, Churchill was heir presumptive to the dukedom.

Churchill had good reason to feel fondness for Blenheim, as an important occasion took place there. It was during the summer of 1908 at the Temple of Diana, designed by Sir William Chambers, in the gardens overlooking the lake that he proposed to Miss Clementine Hozier. She became his devoted wife for 57 years. Churchill was to say later: 'At Blenheim I took two very important decisions: to be born and marry.'

When Sir Winston died in 1965, he was buried beside his parents in the family plot in the churchyard of St Martin's at Bladon, as he had requested; the church tower can be seen from Blenheim. When Lady Churchill died in 1977, her remains were laid to rest in the same grave as those of her husband, which is now marked by a rather brutalist and inaccessible gravestone.

As an untrained architect and much better known as a playwright, John Vanbrugh was a controversial choice as the designer of Marlborough's palace. Wisely, he collaborated with the vastly more qualified and experienced Nicholas Hawksmoor, and he also consulted Christopher Wren. Vanbrugh commented after his commission: 'When the Queen (Anne) declared she would build a house in Woodstock Park for the Duke of Marlborough and she meant it in memory of the great services he had done her and the nation, I found it ought to be considered both as a Royall (sic) and a National Monument and care taken in the design, and the exceution, that it might have the qualitys proper to such a monument, viz, Beauty, Magnificence and Duration.'

Visitors can judge whether Vanbrugh achieved his ambition as they approach the golden Cotswold stone portico, colonnades, turrets and pinnacles of this baroque masterpiece through the 2,100 acres of beautiful parkland, landscaped by 'Capability' Brown in 1764. Brown's Great Lake at Blenheim, created by the damming of the Glyme stream, was described by the poet and art critic Sacheverell Sitwell as 'the one great argument of the landscape gardener. There is nothing finer in Europe.'

Other impressive features in the park include Vanbrugh's classically inspired Grand Bridge over the lake and the 40-m (134-ft) high Column of Victory at the entrance to the Great Avenue. This is topped by a statue of the 1st Duke dressed as a Roman general, with eagles at his feet and a winged Victory in his hand, by Robert Pit. More recent additions have included the Marlborough Maze, said to be the second largest hedged maze in the world, and the Butterfly House.

The monumental East Gate, complete with an inscription giving the story of the construction of the palace, leads to the Clock Tower, which includes Grinling Gibbon's amusing stone-carved representation of British lions savaging French cockerels on either side. The gate opens onto the Great Court, which leads to the main entrance. As you enter the Palace through the two magnificent doors into the Great Hall, the enormous scale of the room – 20m (65ft) high – is balanced by the delicacy of the carvings, many by Grinling Gibbons, and by Sir James Thornhill's exuberant painted ceiling, which shows the 1st Duke of Marlborough presenting his Blenheim strategy to Britannia. Churchill's birthplace is to the right, in a suite of apartments once occupied by the 1st Duke's domestic chaplain.

In addition to the magnificent Nicholas Hawksmoor ceilings and the carvings of Grinling Gibbons, impressive collections of portraits, tapestries and porcelain and exquisite Boulle furniture grace many of the rooms. Highlights include the displays of Meissen and Sèvres porcelain in the China Ante Room, which include the Meissen service presented to the 3rd Duke by the King of Poland in return for a pack of staghounds, and portraits of members of the family in the Green and Red Drawing Rooms and the Green Writing Room.

Taking pride of place in the Green Writing Room is the famous Blenheim Tapestry by the Brussels weaver Judocus de Vos, showing Marlborough in his hour of triumph as he accepts Marshal Tallard's surrender after the Battle of Blenheim in 1704. The tapestry is a superb example of the weaver's art and is the first in a series of ten Victory tapestries that grace the walls of the other state rooms.

The Saloon, with its magnificent ceiling and trompe l'oeil murals by Louis Laguerre, is also known as the State Dining Room and is used by the family once a year on Christmas Day. The three apartments connecting the Saloon and the Long Library on the south front are known as the First, Second and Third State Rooms. A copy of Marlborough's famous dispatch to his wife Sarah, written on the back of a tavern bill from the battlefield at Blenheim (the original is in the British Library), is on display in the First State Room. Also on display here is the Blenheim Standard, which has been sent as quit-rent (in lieu of services) to the sovereign every year on the anniversary of the Battle of Blenheim on 13 August.

For many, Hawksmoor's finest room is the Long Library, in the West Wing of the Palace. A staggering 55m (180ft) long and 10m (32ft) high, it contains 10,000 books collected by the 9th Duke. Originally designed as a picture gallery, the room still displays full-length portraits of Queen Anne, William III and the 1st Duke of Marlborough, but perhaps the most impressive feature is the magnificent Willis organ, installed in 1902.

Right: The formal gardens of Blenheim

Derwent Valley Mills

The Arkwright system substituted capital for labour, machines for skill, factory for home, and mill discipline for family work routines.
David Jeremy, editor, *Transatlantic Industrial Revolution* (1981)

It's difficult to overestimate the effect that Richard Arkwright's pioneering factory system, first introduced to his cotton mills in Derbyshire's Derwent Valley in the late 18th century, had on the industrial life of Britain, and, ultimately, the rest of the world. His use of water power to drive the machinery in his mills, as well as his enlightened sense of responsibility for his workforce in the form of purpose-built housing and community facilities, revolutionized the production and quality of the finished goods, and transformed Britain into a major industrial nation. The Derwent Valley truly became the powerhouse of the Industrial Revolution.

This fact finally received the international recognition it deserved in 2001, when a 15-mile (23-km) corridor along the Derwent Valley, between Derby in the south and Cromford in the north, was inscribed as a World Heritage Site. Included in the area were ten important early industrial sites, most of them the mills that utilized the abundant power of the county's mightiest river, the Derwent. The itinerant journalist and author Daniel Defoe had described the Derwent in his *Tour thro' the Whole Island of Great Britain* in 1726 as 'that fury of a river', and 'a frightful creature when the hills load her current with water…'. And he noted: 'Here is a Curiosity of a very extraordinary Nature, and the only one of the kind in England: I mean those Mills on the Derwent…'

The Derwent mills

The first of these revolutionary mills was the Derby Silk Mill, built between 1702 and 1717 by the engineer George Sorocold, who had earlier been commissioned to supply the town with piped water. The mill was eventually opened in 1721. The massive stone arches, which were its foundations, are still visible, but the rest of the building burned down in 1919. The Derby Museum of Industry and History now stands in its place.

Silk-making in late 17th-century England was founded on the great demand for silk products and the skill of the Huguenot weavers who had fled from France to England to escape religious persecution. Thomas Cotchett, a Derby solicitor, became interested in the commercial possibilities of silk production and turned to Sorocold for his expertise in installing the new, water-powered machinery.

Above: Sluice gate machinery at the East Mill, Belper, with the River Derwent beyond

Cotchett installed a number of 'Dutch machines' (throwing machines, used to spin silk) at a five-storey water-powered mill near the centre of Derby, but the venture was not a success. However, one of the mill's employees, John Lombe, went to Italy, where the highest-quality silk was produced, on a mission of 'industrial espionage', and returned with detailed drawings of Piedmontese throwing machines. These were then copied and successfully installed in the Derby mill, which soon became known as the Italian Works.

Meanwhile, at Cromford in 1771, Richard Arkwright (see box, p.98) extended the range and scale of the mechanization of cotton spinning and factory production techniques, to create the world's first successful water-powered cotton spinning mill. He used the power of Cromford Sough (a sough, pronounced 'suff', is a Derbyshire lead-mining drainage channel), separated from Bonsall Brook, which fed into the Derwent, to operate the machinery in his first five-storey mill, now known as the Upper Mill. The water was brought to an overshot wheel by an aqueduct, unfortunately demolished by a passing lorry in an accident a few years ago.

Arkwright's second mill at Cromford, the Lower Mill, built in 1776–77 and six storeys high, was built after he had perfected the mechanism of the pre-spinning process. This signalled a period of intense expansion for Arkwright, and he followed up his Cromford experiment with more new cotton mills at Bakewell, Wirksworth and Cressbrook.

Above: An 18th-century print of Derby Silk Mill

THE CARDING ENGINE.

The large number of employees attracted to work in Arkwright's cotton mills at Cromford required accommodation and, over the next 20 years, he and his son, also called Richard, provided high-quality housing in places like North Street, Water Lane and Cromford Hill. But the Arkwrights were also concerned with the social and spiritual welfare of their employees, building, among others, the classically pedimented Greyhound Hotel (originally the Black Dog Inn) in Cromford's spacious Market Place; the School and School House in North Street; and St Mary's Church in Mill Lane.

Venetian-windowed and red-bricked Masson Mill on the A6 is testimony to Arkwright's growing wealth and self-confidence. Built on the banks of the Derwent in 1783, it offered ten times the power of his original mills, and the external staircases meant the factory floor was uncluttered – features designed to increase production. Masson Mill is now home to the Sir Richard Arkwright's Masson Working Textile Mills Museum, where you can still see the machinery in place.

The Cromford Canal, built in the early 1790s by William Jessop, assisted by Benjamin Outram, ran for 14 miles (23km) between Cromford and the Erewash Canal at Langley Mill. It was originally intended as a through-route to the fast-expanding industrial city of Manchester. However, it was not until the construction of the Cromford and High Peak Railway between 1824 and 1830, which negotiated the 300-m (1,000-ft) high White Peak plateau with a series of inclined planes, that this dream was realized. It has been said that, were it not for its relative inaccessibility, Cromford might have occupied the same position as Manchester in the country's industrial hierarchy.

Between 1776 and 1815, Arkwright's partner in the first Cromford Mill, Jedediah Strutt, and his sons William, George Benson and Joseph built their first mills at Belper and Milford. Like Arkwright, they also made ample provision for their workforce.

As a result of William Strutt's innovative engineering talents, the range of buildings at Belper charted the evolution of mill design, from traditional stone and timber structures through to the first steps in fire protection using internal iron and brick-arches. Unfortunately, few of the Strutt family's earlier buildings survived the renovations of the 1960s.

Although looking from the outside like any other Arkwright-style mill, Belper North Mill, which was built by William Strutt in 1804 on the lower storeys of another mill partially destroyed by fire the year before, incorporated into its interior the latest ideas on fire protection from the architect Charles Bage. The use of interior plaster cladding and iron columns springing from brick and tile floors drastically reduced the risk of fire. There was also a built-in system of hot-air central heating. Sir Neil

Left: Leawood Pumping Station on the Cromford Canal
Above, top: Jedediah Strutt, Arkwright's business partner in Cromford Mill
Bottom: Engraving of Richard Arkwright's carding machine, invented in 1775

Richard Arkwright started out as a barber and wig-maker in Preston, Lancashire, where he was born in 1732. As he travelled around collecting human hair for his wigs, he came into contact with many home-based spinners and weavers, and began to take an interest in the manufacture of cotton goods. Having no mechanical skills himself, he teamed up with clockmaker John Kay and reed-maker Thomas Highs. Between them, they created the first 'spinning frame'. This led to the idea of a 'water frame', which could be operated by unskilled workers and was powered by water. In partnership with Jedediah Strutt and Samuel Need, inventors of the famous Derby rib silk stocking, he settled on the River Derwent at Cromford as the site of his first purpose-built mill in 1771.

Arkwright was one of the more enlightened of 18th-century industrialists, providing well-built houses, a school and chapel for his workers in Cromford. Even so, two-thirds of his workforce were children, who, from the age of six, worked 13-hour days, by candle- or gaslight at night, as portrayed in Joseph Wright's 1783 painting, *Arkwright's Cotton Mills at Night*.

By 1776, he was employing more than 5,000 people. When he died at the age of 60 in 1792 he left £500,000, equivalent today to around £200m.

Cossons, chairman of English Heritage, has described North Mill as 'the most beautiful, sophisticated and technically perfect structure of its era'.

Travellers on the A6 between Derby and Matlock cannot fail to notice the fortress-like, seven-storey, red-brick structure of Belper's East Mill, which completely overshadows the neighbouring North Mill. Built in 1912 by the English Sewing Company, it incorporated a free-standing, steel frame construction, unlike the wall-supported Strutt mills.

Much of the industrial housing provided by the Strutt family is still evident in the modern town of Belper, including Bridge Foot, Hopping Hill, Belper Lane, King Street and Bridge Street. The design of the housing varies from terrace to terrace, but they are all substantially built gritstone and slate-tiled dwellings, presenting an overall pleasing mixture of styles.

The Strutts also built the Unitarian chapel in Belper in 1787–88; established the Belper Provision Company, an early co-operative enterprise that distributed profits among its customers, in 1821; and insisted on children attending Day Schools and Sunday Schools.

The Dyehouse and chimney at Milford, by the bridge over the River Derwent, is a later development by William Strutt, built in 1832, two years after his death. Its fortress-like, windowless aspect from the A6, like that of the Upper Mill at Cromford, is a reminder of the defensive appearance of some early mills, which were threatened by machine-smashing Luddites, who feared that mechanization would result in the loss of their jobs.

Long Mill, West Mill and East at Darley Abbey are also imposing structures. Although not as well known as those at Cromford, they are among the most complete and intact early cotton factory sites within the World Heritage Site. The five-storey Long Mill was built between 1782 and 1789, and the metal sheathing of its wooden columns was one of the earliest examples of fire protection. The West and East Mills were constructed between 1819 and 1821 by the Evans family, who were in partnership with Richard Arkwright, Junior.

Ironbridge Gorge

If there is one iconic image that symbolizes the beginnings of the Industrial Revolution, it must surely be the deceptively delicate filigree ironwork of the world's first cast-iron bridge. Built in 1779, Iron Bridge springs 30m (100ft) across the turbulent River Severn at Ironbridge in Shropshire. Inscribed in 1985, together with its associated sites spreading along 3 miles (5km) of the River Severn gorge between Coalbrookdale and Coalport, the bridge is the focal point of the Ironbridge Gorge World Heritage Site.

Ironbridge and Coalbrookdale were the crucibles of the Industrial Revolution, changing Britain forever from a largely rural nation to an industrial one, and lighting a flame that was to spread around the world. Shrewsbury cotton master Charles Hulbert described Ironbridge in 1837 as 'the most extraordinary district in the world'. Set within the dramatic natural landscape of the River Severn gorge, with steep, hanging woodlands interspersed with grassy meadows, it includes the settlements of Madeley, Coalport, Jackfield and Benthall.

The fame of Ironbridge is inextricably tied up with the fortunes of the Darby family, three generations of Quakers who created the world's first industrial complex. Abraham Darby I (1678–1717), the dynasty's founder and the son of a Staffordshire Quaker, served an apprenticeship to a mill-maker in Birmingham, then set up as a brass-founder in Bristol. He later moved to Coalbrookdale, where he developed the revolutionary technique of smelting iron with coke, instead of charcoal, at the Old Furnace in 1709. His son, Abraham Darby II, perfected the technique and developed better-quality castings – thus providing another great impetus in the Industrial Revolution. But perhaps the most famous of the Darby dynasty was Abraham Darby III (1750–91), who took over the family business in the 1770s. He was responsible for creating the world's first cast-iron bridge, across the River Severn, in 1779.

Like many Quakers, Abraham III appears to have been an enlightened employer. In times of food shortages, he bought up failing local farms to grow food for his workers, built good-quality housing for them, and offered higher wages than those paid in other local industries. He died aged only 41 years old.

In the *Annals of Agriculture* of 1785, Arthur Young vividly described the following scene: 'Colebrook (sic) Dale itself is a very romantic spot, it is a winding glen between two immense hills which break into various forms, and all thickly covered with wood, forming the most beautiful sheets of hanging wood. Indeed too beautiful to be much in unison with that variety of horrors art has spread at the bottom: the noise of the forges, mills, &. with all their vast machinery, the flames bursting from the furnaces with the burning of the coal and the smoak (sic) of the lime kilns, are altogether sublime…'

The Iron Bridge

The iconic Iron Bridge was the brainchild of Abraham Darby III, who wanted to link the parishes of Madeley and Benthall on opposite sides of the Severn. It was designed by the Shrewsbury architect Thomas Farnolls Pritchard. You can still see the wood-panelled study in Dale House, Coalbrookdale, where Darby worked on his plans for the revolutionary bridge, which cost a mere £6,000 at the time. It was officially opened to scenes of great festivity on New Year's Day, 1781.

The bridge has five, 5.25-tonne arched ribs, each of which were cast in two halves at Darby's Coalbrookdale foundry just downstream of Dale House. It is made up of a complicated jigsaw of about 800 castings of a dozen different types. It has been claimed that the traditional woodworking methods employed, such as the use of dovetail and mortice-and-tenon joints, accounted for the bridge's remarkable longevity and stability between the shifting banks of the Severn. It's worth noting that woodworking was still the most advanced construction technique at the time.

Soon after the opening of the bridge, ancient Madeley market was relocated to a new purpose-built Square in what is now the town of Ironbridge. It gave the formerly scattered settlement of Madeley Wood a new focus and a new name, and Ironbridge soon became the commercial and administrative centre of the Coalbrookdale area. The Iron Bridge shareholders also built the Tontine Hotel in 1784 to accommodate the many visitors, including artists and rival engineers, flocking to see the new bridge and other pioneering industrial sites of the Severn gorge. At the opposite end of the bridge from the hotel is the old Toll House, complete with a list of Victorian tolls required to cross it posted on a notice outside: 2s (10p) to cross with a six-horse carriage; 1s (5p) for a coach-and-four; and a halfpenny for a calf, pig, sheep or lamb – or a pedestrian. The Toll House now serves as the Ironbridge Tourist Information Centre.

The Museum of the Gorge, close to the bridge itself, is one of a family of ten museums in the World Heritage Site. It tells the story of the bridge, illustrated by audio-visual displays and a huge scale model of how it looked in its heyday in 1796.

Left and overleaf: Telford's iconic Iron Bridge across the River Severn

The beginnings of a revolution

A number of factors combined in the rise of Coalbrookdale and Ironbridge as the birthplace of industrial Britain. Chief among these was the abundant presence of the raw materials needed for the production of iron – namely coal, ironstone, clay and wood. Another vitally important consideration was the River Severn, which provided both power and transportation.

But perhaps even more significant was the presence in the area of a group of highly imaginative and innovative entrepreneurs and engineers. People such as the Darby family (see box, p.101), John Wilkinson, William Reynolds and Thomas Telford were all linked with the area, and there remains much evidence of their influence in the buildings and settlements of Ironbridge Gorge.

It was a number of years earlier in 1709, at the Old Furnace in Coalbrookdale, that Abraham Darby I first developed the revolutionary technique of smelting iron ore with coke instead of charcoal, which made the production of iron much cheaper. His grandson, Abraham Darby III, later used the technique for building the Iron Bridge. In 2009, the 300th anniversary of coke smelting was celebrated by a series of events at the Ironbridge Gorge Museum.

The furnace used water stored in the Upper Furnace Pool, a reservoir used to power a waterwheel and operate the bellows, creating the great heat necessary to smelt the ore. The furnace was charged from above with alternate layers of coke and iron ore, to which limestone was added. The limestone melted and impurities were run off separately as slag.

When sufficient iron had accumulated in the hearth, the furnace was tapped and iron was allowed to flow out for making pig iron or iron castings. The furnace remained in use until the 1820s, when the subsequent development of the Coalbrookdale site swallowed it up in later workshops. However, in the 1950s, it was rediscovered and restored, and in the 1980s a protective cover was built over it.

The economy of Ironbridge Gorge was based on the industries of mining, iron and ceramics. With the exception of the Coalbrookdale Works of the Aga-Rayburn company, manufacturers of the world-famous range-style cookers and cookware and located on one of the original foundry sites of Abraham Darby I, these have long since disappeared.

Today the Great Warehouse at Coalbrookdale houses the Museum of Iron, and you can still see the original furnace where Abraham Darby III smelted the iron used in the construction of the Iron Bridge. Other exhibits and models explain the process

in great detail, including a collection of fine-art castings. An adjacent building houses Enginuity – an interactive design and technology centre, which aims to show the secrets of how everyday things are made and how they work.

The different levels of houses clinging to the hillside show how the class system worked in Georgian and Victorian times. The poorer classes lived lower down the valley, with the grander houses of the ironmasters, such as Rosehill House and Dale House where the Darbys lived, at the top of the hill, giving commanding views of the gorge.

There have been pottery and tile works in the busy Severn-side port of Jackfield from the 17th-century to the present day. At first, the area was known for its drinking mugs, and by the middle of the 18th century, black-decorated Jackfield earthenware was being produced. But it was the Victorian tile factories of Maw and Company (1883) and Craven Dunnill (1874), both producing highly decorative and glazed tiles, which really gave Jackfield its name and made it the most important centre in the world for the manufacture of tiles.

The Jackfield Tile Museum, housed in Henry Powell Dunnill's former factory, is the best-surviving example of a purpose-built Victorian tile factory. Decorative tiles, many of which are on display, were produced here from 1874 until just after World War II. In addition to their most encountered use – in public toilets – they also decorated royal palaces and many public buildings in Britain's fast-expanding colonial empire.

The large open-air complex of the Blists Hill Victorian Town, by the Shropshire Canal above the gorge at Madeley, is one of the site's most popular attractions. Operated by the Ironbridge Museum Trust, Blists Hill is a living time capsule, transporting you back to the 19th-century heyday of Ironbridge and the surrounding area.

All the staff are dressed in authentic period costume, and many are specially trained to demonstrate the crafts and trades of the industrial past. You can enter the shops and houses of the 'residents', including a printer, candle-maker and blacksmith, and really experience what life was like for the employees of the Darbys through the years. You can even enjoy a pint at an authentic village pub.

The Shropshire Canal was linked to the River Severn by the famous Hay Inclined Plane. This was constructed in 1793 by Henry Williams and James Loudon to raise boats up over 60m (200ft) on a 1 in 4 gradient from the river to the canal. An ingenious system where the canal boats were placed in wheeled cradles and raised under steam power on wooden rails was devised. The total distance was 305m (330 yards), and the inclined plane supposedly did the work of 27 locks. Not only was it three times faster than a system of locks, it needed only four men to operate it. The last lift took place

Top: Blists Hill Victorian Town
Centre: Early English tile designs
Bottom: Coalport China Museum

SEVERN CORACLES

SEVERN CORACLES

If you are very lucky on the day of your visit to Ironbridge, you may see one of the ancient, small, round-bottomed boats known as coracles being sculled across the River Severn.

A coracle consists of a wicker frame covered in cowhide, with a single plank seat in the middle. The difficult tasks of propulsion and manoeuvring are achieved with just a single paddle, and it is an education to see one of these flimsy, inherently unstable crafts in the hands of an expert.

The cowhides used for the outer shell are carefully selected, cured and waterproofed, and willow and hazel wands tied with horsehair twine are used for the frame of the boat. As it dries out, the cowhide 'skin' shrinks tightly around the frame to make the boat waterproof and river-worthy.

As well as being used by local people over the centuries for fishing or simply for crossing the river, coracles were also very effective emergency vessels, rescuing animals or people from floods and even finding bodies after an accident or suicide.

Eustace Rogers, the last in a long family line of Ironbridge coracle-makers, died in his 90th year in 2003.

in 1894, with the Hay Inclined Plane officially closing in 1907. Today, there is a public footpath leading up one side of the incline.

Near the base of the incline is Coalport's Tar Tunnel, one of the rarest and strangest mineral mines in the country. Workmen digging a new canal tunnel in 1787 noticed a sticky black substance leaking out of the walls, forming pools inside the tunnel. When it was realized that this was bitumen, large cauldrons were built to convert it into pitch. It was then used to waterproof wooden ships, ropes and roofs and to make lampblack.

Previously, bitumen had to be exported from the West Indies and North and South America, so its accidental discovery made the tunnel an immediate economic success. At its busiest, it yielded up to 440 gallons (2,000 litres) a day, but by 1820, production was down to ten barrels a year and it ceased altogether in 1843. The tunnel was rediscovered in 1964, opened to the public in 1973, and today you can still see the black tar oozing from the walls.

The town of Coalport was the vision of ironmaster William Reynolds in the late 18th century, who saw it as a hub for the iron industry and built factories and accommodation for his workers. The coming of the Shropshire Canal and the link via the Hay Inclined Plane was the key to the success of his plan. But Coalport's real claim to fame came when Reynolds tempted John Rose to move from Jackfield to found a china and porcelain factory there in 1792.

By the early 1800s Rose's superb porcelain was attracting worldwide attention. One of his workers was Thomas Minton, who eventually left and set up his own business making the famous Mintonware in Staffordshire. China was made on the site from 1792 until 1926, when Coalport China became part of the Wedgwood empire and it followed Minton to the Potteries of Staffordshire.

Rose's former Coalport China Works is now the Coalport China Museum, which, among other things, displays the National Collections of Caughley and Coalport China. Daily demonstrations of china-making can be seen in the workshops, and visitors can purchase examples of all the work in the museum shop.

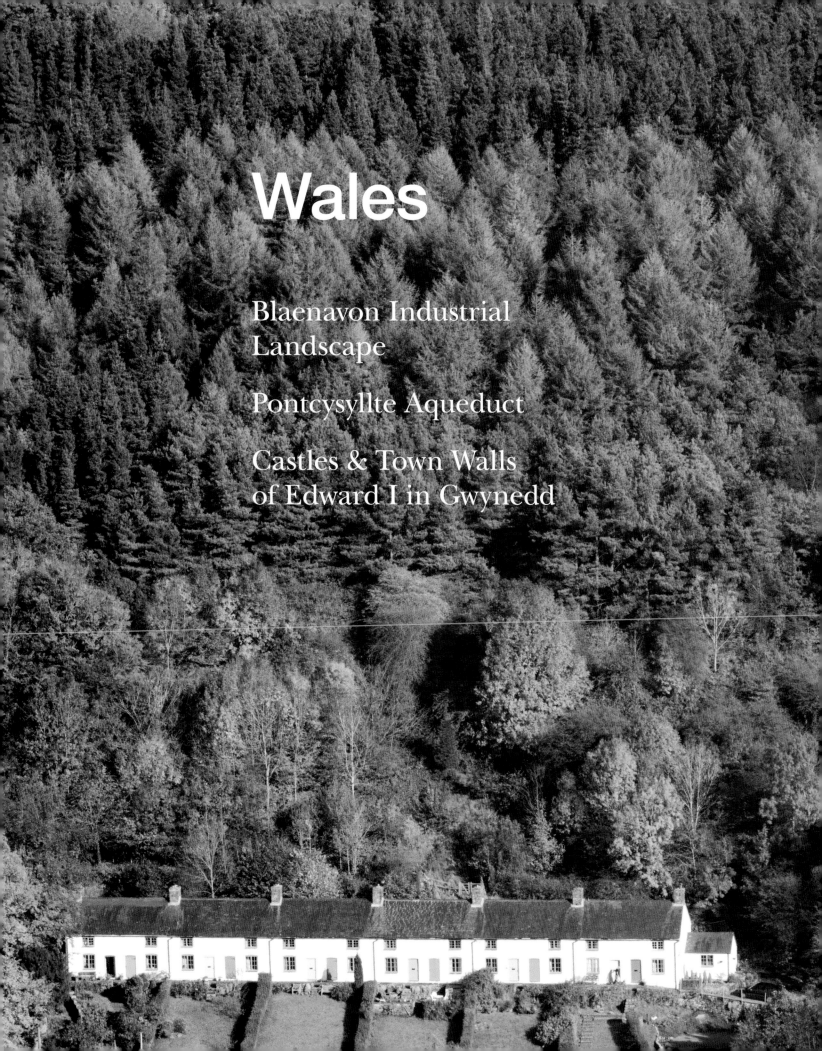

Wales

Blaenavon Industrial
Landscape

Pontcysyllte Aqueduct

Castles & Town Walls
of Edward I in Gwynedd

Blaenavon Industrial Landscape

At some distance, the works have the appearance of a small town, surrounded with heaps of ore, coal and limestone, and enlivened with all the bustle and activity of an opulent and increasing establishment... Although these works were only finished in 1789, three hundred and fifty men are employed, and the population of the district exceeds a thousand souls.
Archdeacon William Coxe of Wiltshire (1747–1828)

This eyebrow-raising description, written by the experienced traveller Coxe on a visit to Blaenavon at the end of the 18th century, reflects the revolutionary nature of the industrial landscape. At the time, Blaenavon was the world's largest centre for the production of iron and coal. Industry on this scale had never been seen before in the Welsh valleys, and what happened here in the 100 years or so from 1789 was to change the face of British industry and, later, that of the entire industrial world. Blaenavon's pioneering industrial landscape was inscribed as a World Heritage Site in 2000, in recognition of its position as the world's first major production site for iron and coal. The WHS encompasses the ironworks, probably the best-preserved example from the 19th century in the world, the coal mines and the community housing built by the ironmasters for their workers.

Lord Abergavenny's Hills

As so often happens, geology was the foundation of Blaenavon's fortune. The readily available supplies of coal, limestone and iron ore were the essential raw materials needed for the large-scale production of iron. The area around Blaenavon, originally named Lord Abergavenny's Hills after its landlord, was rich in these minerals and natural resources. Three industrialists from the West Midlands – Thomas Hill, Thomas Hopkins and Benjamin Pratt – took over the lease on 12,000 acres of land from Lord Abergavenny in 1789. The Blaenavon Ironworks opened in the same year, constructed at the then enormous cost of £40,000. The three original blast furnaces employed about 300 men, many of whom were experienced iron-workers who had followed their employers from the Midlands. Before long, the ironworks were producing several thousand tonnes of pig iron every year.

The South Wales iron industry developed at a time of vastly increased demand for iron goods. Britain was involved in several overseas wars, including the American War of Independence and the French Revolutionary and Napoleonic Wars, and iron was essential for the manufacture of armaments, cannon balls and other weapons.

The demand for iron rails to feed the rail network that was spreading rapidly across Britain during the early 19th century also appeared insatiable, and, eventually, a new forge was constructed in the village of Garnddyrys, close to Blaenavon, to satisfy the demand. By 1796, Blaenavon's annual output of iron was 4,318 tonnes. Due to increasing demand, coupled with technological improvements such as the installation of a Boulton and Watt engine in 1800, and the creation of a new blast furnace in 1805, annual production rose to over 14,000 tonnes by 1812. At the time, this was the highest in Wales. By the early 19th century, Hill, Hopkins and Pratt had also started developing the model town of Blaenavon for their workers. The population was rising fast, as workers from the Midlands, Ireland and Scotland flocked to the town to share in the benefits provided by the prospering iron industry.

Scottish industrialist Robert William Kennard took over the Blaenavon Company during the 1840s, shortly after it had been set up as a joint stock company. Kennard's family dominated the company for many years, but it was Nottinghamshire-born James Ashwell, a pupil of the great engineer Bryan Donkin, who was responsible for the most extensive programme of improvements to the company's housing, furnaces, forges and transport.

The most impressive existing monument to Ashwell's work at Blaenavon is the neo-classical, temple-like water balance tower, which was built in 1839. This lift technology, where the weight of water counterbalances the loads, was used in the mine shafts of

Above: An old explosives truck at Blaenavon
Overleaf: Garn yr Erw near Big Pit, Blaenavon

South Wales and at several other ironworks, but the Blaenavon tower is the best surviving example. The lift tower was linked to the high ground behind it by a wooden bridge – this was eventually replaced by a stone bridge, which still remains. Its winding gear consisted of a cast-iron frame with classical detailing. On this was mounted a pulley wheel, over which a chain linked a pair of lift cages, each incorporating a wrought-iron water tank. By piping water in or out of the tank, wagons could be lifted or lowered as required. The stonework is of the highest quality and, topped by the remnants of the cast-iron frame, the tower resembles a ruined Grecian temple.

Originally known as Kearsley's Pit, Big Pit is now home to the National Coal Museum of Wales. An amalgamation of several mines, Big Pit was, however, for a century the most important colliery in the town, and one of a number operating in the Blaenavon area during the 19th and 20th centuries. The first shaft at Big Pit was sunk in 1860 by the Blaenavon Company to a depth of 60m (200ft). The name of Big Pit was given to the mine because of this unusually large elliptical shaft, which was deepened still further in 1880 to 90m (300ft). The mine eventually closed in 1980.

You can get a taste of what life was like for the miners at Big Pit by taking an underground tour, many of which are led by former miners. You are lowered in a cage to the foot of the 1860 shaft, just as the miners were, and shown some of the earliest workings. Many mines in the Blaenavon area, including Forge Level, one of the earliest workings in Big Pit, were originally used for the extraction of iron ore rather than coal. However, by the late 19th century, Welsh steel- and iron-making was on the wane, and was replaced by 'King Coal', as the South Wales Coalfield was known at the height of its production.

Left: Blast furnace at Blaenavon
Right: Row of miners' cottages at Stack Square

Gradually, the original Blaenavon Ironworks began to lose its importance. The new steelworks at nearby Forgeside was completed during the 1860s and the old site was allowed to fall into disrepair. Production at the North Street ironworks ceased completely during the early 1900s and the site became used as a maintenance yard for the company's collieries and steelworks.

A growing demand for Welsh coal to fuel locomotives, steamships and factories and to heat houses meant that many South Wales towns, including Blaenavon, began to specialize in the production of coal. The Big Pit employed some 1,300 men during the early 1920s, and Blaenavon coal was shipped around the world, as far away as South America. The Blaenavon Ironworks was scheduled for demolition in 1970 but, fortunately, the site was taken into state care in 1974 and saved. From 1974, a programme of excavation, consolidation and repair was begun. The work was carried out to emphasize the site's authenticity as a consolidated ruin, preserving all its surviving features. No reconstruction took place, except where necessary for structural purposes, and, wherever possible, all conservation measures were devised to be reversible. Since 2008, the Blaenavon Ironworks and the cottages at Stack Square in the town have been under the direct management of Cadw, the historic environment service of the Welsh government.

Blaenavon Town

Visitors might recognize Stack Square and Engine Row at Blaenavon as the setting for BBC TV's *Coal House* series. The houses form a small group of solidly built stone cottages, incorporating patterns of building, notably for the doors and window-heads, that are characteristic of Hill, Hopkins and Pratt's native West Midlands. The houses were erected during the 1780s by the ironmasters for the first skilled workers who operated their furnaces. They form a courtyard into which a 50-m (164-ft) high chimney stack for a new engine house was placed in 1860, the base of which can still be seen. The central range of the courtyard was originally the company office, shop and manager's house, but this was converted to much smaller houses than the skilled workers' homes on either side of them in the 1860s. Stack Square is a Scheduled Ancient Monument. Other features of the town include the parish church of St Peter, built in 1804 in the Gothic Revival style by Hill and Hopkins, and the many Nonconformist chapels, with stirring biblical names such as Bethlehem, Moriah and Horeb. Not only were these religious centres for the community and the home of some fine choirs, they were also educational facilities. But perhaps the most impressive building in Blaenavon is the Workmen's Hall and Institute, which opened in 1895. To build it, a total of £10,000 was raised by a levy of a halfpenny a week deducted from the wages of the workforce. As well as a library, a reading room and games rooms, this forerunner of the working men's club included a stage for lectures and concerts.

Right: Pit head winding gear of the Big Pit

Pontcysyllte Aqueduct

Tuesday, 26 November 1805 was a very special day in the history of the peaceful Deeside villages of Froncysyllte and Trevor, 3 miles (4.8km) upstream from Llangollen in North Wales. Just a month after the news of Nelson's historic victory at the Battle of Trafalgar, more than 8,000 people thronged into the valley to witness the official opening of the Pontcysyllte Aqueduct, heralded as a wonder of the age.

The aqueduct, which formed a key link in the Ellesmere (now the Llangollen) Canal, had taken around ten years to design and build, and cost £47,000 (£2.8 million today). The iron and masonry structure soared majestically for more than 300m (1,000ft) over the Dee at the dizzying height of 38m (126ft), and was the longest and highest cast-iron aqueduct in the world. Conceived by the celebrated civil engineer Thomas Telford, nicknamed the 'Colossus of Roads' by his friend, the poet Robert Southey, and assisted by experienced canal engineer William Jessop, it was, and still is, a pioneering masterpiece of civil engineering and monumental canal architecture.

Prompted by a signal from a cannon fired by the Royal Artillery on a platform in the valley below, the first two narrowboats, carrying the management committee and their families, crossed the aqueduct on that epic day two centuries ago. A third boat carried the band of the Shropshire Volunteers in full-dress uniform, while a fourth

Above: Thomas Telford
Right: The Pontcysyllte Aqueduct, built by
Thomas Telford in 1795

carried the civil engineers who had built the aqueduct. The last two boats had a symbolic cargo of coal, representing the first commercial use of the aqueduct.

A plaque unveiled on one of the piers read: 'The nobility and gentry of the adjacent counties having united their efforts with the great commercial interest of this country in creating an intercourse and union between England and North Wales. By navigable communication of the three rivers – Severn, Dee and Mersey – for the mutual benefit of agriculture and trade, caused the first stone of the aqueduct of Pontcysyllte to be laid, on the 25th July, 1795, when Richard Myddleton, MP of Chirk, one of the original patrons of the Ellesmere Canal was Lord of the Manor and in the reign of our sovereign George III.'

Today, Pontcysyllte still carries over 15,000 narrowboats every year, and it's one of the region's biggest tourist attractions, attracting an annual 250,000 visitors by boat. It is a Grade I listed building, a Welsh National Monument and, officially, one of the Seven Wonders of the British Waterways system.

The aqueduct and 11 miles (18km) of the canal from Rhoswiel in Shropshire to the Horseshoe Falls near Llangollen (including the older but smaller Chirk Aqueduct, built by Telford in 1801) were inscribed as a World Heritage Site in 2009. The UNESCO citation read: 'The Pontcysyllte Aqueduct is a pioneering masterpiece of engineering and monumental architecture by the famous civil engineer Thomas Telford.'

How the aqueduct was built

Telford's aim with the Ellesmere Canal was to link the ironworks and collieries of Wrexham with Chester, via the northwest Shropshire town of Ellesmere and utilizing the existing Chester Canal and the River Mersey. Despite considerable public scepticism, Telford was confident the construction method he had envisaged to cross the valley of the Dee at Pontcysyllte would work. He had previously built two cast-iron trough aqueducts: the Chirk Aqueduct across the Ceiriog Valley, also on the Ellesmere Canal, and the Longdon-on-Tern aqueduct on the Shrewsbury Canal.

His Pontcysyllte masterpiece consists of a 3.4-m (11-ft) wide and 1.6-m (5.25-ft) deep cast-iron trough, supported above the river on iron arched ribs carried on 19 hollow masonry piers. Each span is 16m (53ft) wide, and the mortar used for the piers was made up of lime, water and ox blood.

The iron castings for the aqueduct's trough were supplied by William Hazledine from his foundries at Shrewsbury and the nearby Plas Kynaston Foundry at Cefn Mawr, which was built for the purpose. The trough itself was made from flanged plates of

cast iron, bolted together, with the joints caulked with Welsh flannel and a mixture of white lead and iron particles. The plates are not rectangular but shaped to give the impression of traditional stone voussoirs (wedges), continuing the line of the arch ribs beneath. The supporting arches, four for each span, are made up of cast-iron ribs, with infill panels on the outside to give the appearance of stone supports. The trough is not fastened to the arches – lugs cast into the 'floor' plates fit over the ribs to prevent movement – and it was apparently left for six months with water inside to check that it was watertight.

The vertiginous towpath is cantilevered out from the side of the trough, which allows the trough to take up the maximum width of the piers. Water displaced by the passage of a narrowboat can then flow around the boat, giving free passage for the walker or horse, the original motive power for the narrowboats, on the path. It's still an exciting experience to navigate a narrowboat across the aqueduct, and even more nerve-wracking to walk the towpath! Walkers are protected by railings on the outside edge of the towpath, but the holes to fit railings on the other side of the aqueduct were, for some reason, never used. On the other side, the edge of the trough is only about 15cm (6in) above the water level, well below the deck of a narrowboat. This means there is nothing between the navigator of a narrowboat and the River Dee 38m (125ft) below. Every five years, a plug in the centre of the aqueduct is opened to drain the canal, so that maintenance can take place. This results in a spectacular waterfall that cascades into the River Dee.

Whe he put forward the Pontcysyllte aqueduct and canal for WHS nomination, the then culture secretary James Purnell said: 'The Pontcysyllte Aqueduct and Canal is truly a masterpiece from the canal age in the UK. It is also a magnificent example of our living heritage, remaining one of the busiest stretches of canal in the UK.'

Left: A narrowboat crosses the Pontcysyllte Aqueduct

Castles & Town Walls of Edward I in Gwynedd

The purpose of the castles was to terrify the Welsh into submission, to frighten those already defeated so they would not rise, and to provide the Welsh with a permanent reminder of who was master of their land.

Plantagenet Somerset Fry, *Castles of Britain and Ireland*, 1996

King Edward I's invasion, conquest and suppression of Wales, which took place between 1277 and 1295, was typical of this ruthless monarch, known not only for his height (his nickname was Longshanks) but also for his intimidating and temperamental nature.

Wales had long been England's troublesome neighbour. The Welsh Prince of Wales, Llywelyn ap Gruffydd, had been in constant conflict with the English marcher (border) lords, and these problems were exacerbated when Dafydd, Llywelyn's younger brother, and Gruffydd ap Gwenwynwyn of Powys failed to assassinate him and so defected to the English in 1274. Citing these ongoing hostilities and the fact that Edward I was now harbouring his bitter enemies, Llywelyn refused to do homage to him. A further provocation for Edward came when Llywelyn announced his intention to marry Eleanor, daughter of Simon de Montfort, Edward's old enemy.

In November 1276, Edward declared war on Wales and, in July 1277, he invaded with a force of 15,500, of whom 9,000 were Welsh. The campaign never became a major battle – local support for Llywelyn was weak and he soon realized he had no choice but to surrender. Under the Treaty of Aberconwy in November 1277, Llywelyn was left only with the land of Gwynedd, in the far north of the country, but he was allowed to retain the title of Prince of Wales.

War broke out again in 1282, provoked by Edward's attempts to impose English law on his Welsh subjects. Unlike the previous uprising, this time the conflict enjoyed wide support from the Welsh. For Edward, it became a war of conquest, rather than simply a punitive expedition, like his previous campaign.

In 1284, the Statute of Rhuddlan incorporated the principality of Wales into England, and Wales was given an administrative system like the English, with counties policed by sheriffs. English law was introduced in criminal cases, although the Welsh were allowed to retain their own laws in some property disputes.

Above: Llywelyn ap Gruffydd

Overleaf: Caernarfon Castle in early morning light, seen from the south side

Under Madog ap Llywelyn, a distant relative of Llywelyn ap Gruffydd, further rebellions occurred in 1287–8 and 1294–5. These last conflicts demanded that the king take action, and both rebellions were savagely quashed.

After 1277, and increasingly after 1283, Edward embarked on a full-scale English settlement of Wales, creating planned new towns like Flint, Aberystwyth and Rhuddlan. He also initiated an extensive project of castle-building, designed to subdue the vexatious Welsh. The assignment was given to Master James of St George. He was one of the foremost castle-builders in Europe, whom Edward had met in Savoy on his return from the Ninth Crusade to the Holy Land. Master James was appointed Master of the King's Works in around 1282 and paid the princely rate of 3s (15p) a day, plus a pension of 1s 6d (7.5p) a day for his wife Ambrosia.

The unprecedented scale of Edward's castle-building in Gwynedd is hard to comprehend today. It cost the Exchequer nearly £80,000 in the years between 1277 and 1304 – the equivalent today of about £40 million. And the effects were felt not only in Wales, as Edward press-ganged craftsmen and labourers from all over England to carry out the work. Records show that, for example, 100 diggers and 20 carpenters were enlisted from far-off Norfolk, and 150 diggers, 40 carpenters and 20 masons from Yorkshire. A total of 150 masons, 400 carpenters, 1,000 diggers and 8,000 woodcutters for clearing the land were employed between 1282 and 1283. This scale of military construction was not matched until Henry VIII's programme of coastal fortifications in the mid-16th century – but, in that case, they were guarding against foreign invasion. Within 50 years, however, many of Edward's Welsh castles were in a state of decay and requiring considerable attention.

Among Edward's most important castles in his Gwynedd 'ring of steel' were Beaumaris, Caernarfon, Conwy and Harlech. These form the basis of the Castles and Town Walls of Edward I World Heritage Site, which was inscribed in 1986. All four are now in the care of Cadw and open to the public.

Master James was heavily influenced by eastern architecture, which he had seen during the Crusades, and he drew on it for Edward's massive castle-building programme in Gwynedd. He introduced, for example, arrow slits, the concentric castle at Beaumaris and Harlech, a design never used in Britain before, and distinct echoes of Byzantine architecture at Caernarfon.

In 1284, King Edward's son Edward – later Edward II – was born at Caernarfon Castle. It was here, too, in 1301 that the young Edward was the first English prince to be invested with the title of Prince of Wales (see box, left).

Caernarfon Castle

It's no coincidence that the imposing curtain walls of Caernarfon Castle bear more than a passing resemblance to the fifth-century walls of the golden city of Constantinople in Asia Minor. Edward I had spent some time in the Byzantine capital while taking part in the Ninth Crusade. No doubt, he was impressed by the high curtain walls, built by the Byzantine Emperor Theodosius II, with their banded masonry, punctuated with polygonal, round and square towers.

The site Edward chose for this castle was a key strategic one, overlooking and guarding the Menai Straits. The tidal waters also meant that the castle could be supplied from the sea if it were under siege. Edward chose Caernarfon as his headquarters in Wales not only because it had been the Welsh and Norman capital but also that of the Romans, who built their legionary fortress of Segontium in the same location. The original Norman motte and bailey castle was at the eastern, higher end of the castle enclosure. This is now the main entrance, through the Queen's Gate, a twin polygonal-towered gatehouse that is reached by a ramp up to the drawbridge.

Although Edward's castle at Caernarfon is the grandest and most sophisticated of all his Welsh castles, it is constructed on a simple figure-of-eight, or hourglass, plan. The water-gate access is via the huge polygonal Eagle Tower in the west, which got its name from the carved eagles that once topped its three turrets.

The building work at Caernarfon fell into two main periods: the west, south and east curtain walls and towers, and the Queen's Gate were built between 1283 and 1292; the north side, with the great King's Gate, was added, although never quite completed, between 1296 and 1323. The second stage of building followed repair work needed after the severe and extensive damage caused in the attack on the castle by Madog ap Llywelyn during his rebellion of 1294–5. The castle formed part of larger defensive works by Edward, which saw a fortified wall and towers built around the medieval town, little of which remains today.

Conwy Castle and Walls

Professor Allen Brown, the distinguished medieval scholar and former chair in Medieval History at King's College, London, described Conwy Castle as one of the 'finest and noblest castles in Western Europe and Latin Christendom'.

Like Caernarfon, Conwy was designed by Edward's trusted Master James of St George, and it was built remarkably quickly between 1283 and 1287. Over 1,500 men were recorded as working on its construction in the summer of 1285. The total cost came to nearly £20,000 – or over £10 million in today's money – which made it the most expensive of Edward's Welsh castles.

Right: Telford's suspension bridge of
1822 leading to Conwy Castle

An almost perfect structure of high and thick curtain walls with eight cylindrical flanking towers, Conwy has been described by medieval castle expert Plantagenet Somerset Fry as 'the most compact agglomerate of turretry in the British Isles'. Master James tailored Conwy Castle to fit exactly the rocky promontory guarding the entrance to the River Conwy. He designed a vast enclosure divided into an inner and outer ward, separated by a thick wall. At each end of the wall, there were eight massive, 21-m (70-ft) high, 9-m (30-ft) diameter flanking towers, themselves with walls 4.5m (15ft) thick.

The castle was connected to the walled town of Conwy, also built by Edward. Its impressive turrets were faithfully echoed in Robert Stephenson's first-ever, wrought-iron tubular railway bridge, adjacent to the castle. Designed by William Fairbairn, the bridge opened in 1849. Next to it is Thomas Telford's 1826 suspension bridge, which was designed to echo the turrets of the castle.

During Madog ap Llywelyn's uprising in 1294–5, King Edward established his base at Conwy. But he was no sooner inside the walls than the waters of the Conwy river rose, trapping him inside his great castle. Edward spent many anxious days waiting for the water to subside, his temper no doubt not improved by his enforced diet of salted meat, suspect water and coarse bread.

Within a generation of its building, however, Conwy Castle was unused and began to crumble. It was lived in during the 14th century and, strangely, its apparent impregnability was not tested until the Civil War (1642–51). In 1609, it had been described in an official report as 'utterly decayed' and was sold for £100 (just under £10,000 in today's money).

Beaumaris Castle

Situated on flat, marshy land in the south of the island of Anglesey, Beaumaris Castle was the last of the castles built by Edward I. Its almost perfectly concentric, moated design was thought to be impregnable but this was never put to the test, as no shot appears ever to have been fired at Beaumaris in anger.

In the summer of 1295, about 3,500 workmen from all over England were recorded as working on the castle. But despite that enormous workforce – the equivalent of 1 in 1,000 of the population – and over 35 years of construction, Beaumaris was never completed. Work finally stopped in around 1330, with the final cost estimated at £15,000 – or nearly £7 million today.

The building of Beaumaris – the name means 'fair marsh' – was prompted by Madog ap Llywelyn's uprising in 1294–5. Edward instructed Master James to construct the four-ringed defences, including a water-filled moat, to control the northern shores of the Menai Straits, but in any event none of the towers and gatehouses was built to their full height.

Remarkably, a letter from Master James to the Treasurer and Barons of the Exchequer written in February 1296 still survives. In it, he pleads for more money to complete the work at Beaumaris: '… when this letter was written we were short of £500, for both workmen and the garrison. The men's pay has been and is still very much in arrears, and we are having the greatest difficulty in keeping them because they simply have nothing to live on… if our lord the king wants the work to be finished as quickly as it should be on the scale on which it has commenced, we could not make do with less than £250 a week throughout the season…' It seems that poor Master James never got his money.

Left: Conwy Castle
Above: Aerial view of Beaumaris castle

Harlech Castle

The four square grey towers and walls of Harlech Castle on its lofty crag are a commanding presence when seen from across the blue waters of Tremadog Bay, just as they have been for over seven centuries.

Harlech was one of Master James's most splendid creations, and Edward I rewarded him by granting him the well-paid post of its constable after work was completed in 1290. It took 1,000 men to build the castle in the remarkably short time of seven years, between 1283 and 1290, at a cost of £9,000 (nearly £5 million today).

It's hard to imagine now but, when Harlech Castle was built, the sheer rock face on the west side sloped directly down to the sea of Tremadog Bay, making it approachable only by boat. In the intervening seven centuries, the sea has receded and the land has been reclaimed. What was then water is now salt marsh and sand dunes, with holiday flats and chalets. The remains of the castle sea gate can still be seen at the extreme northern end of the west side.

The dominant feature of Harlech Castle, seen by all visitors as they approach it from the town, is the massive gatehouse set in the east inner wall. This keep-like, three-storeyed structure measures 24m (80ft) by 16m (54ft), with walls 3 to 4m (9 to 12ft) thick. Alongside the twin cylindrical towers flanking the entrance, there were three portcullises and three sets of doors.

Harlech's defences were put to the test by Welsh rebels led by Madog ap Llywelyn in 1294, and the castle garrison of only 37 men successfully beat off the concerted Welsh assault. But then, like so many of Edward's fortresses, once the Welsh uprisings had ceased, the castle was allowed to fall into disrepair.

It was attacked again by the Welsh freedom fighter Owain Glyndwr (c.1349–1416) in the early 15th century. After besieging the castle for many months, eventually starving the garrison out, Glyndwr moved in and set up his headquarters. He may even have held his second-ever Welsh Parliament in the castle.

In 1409, Henry VI sent a strong force under Gilbert Talbot against Harlech. After a short siege, the Welsh garrison surrendered and Glyndwr's family were captured. The elusive Glyndwr managed to slip away, but the fall of Harlech marked the end of his uprising.

Right: Harlech Castle in evening light, with Snowdonia in the background

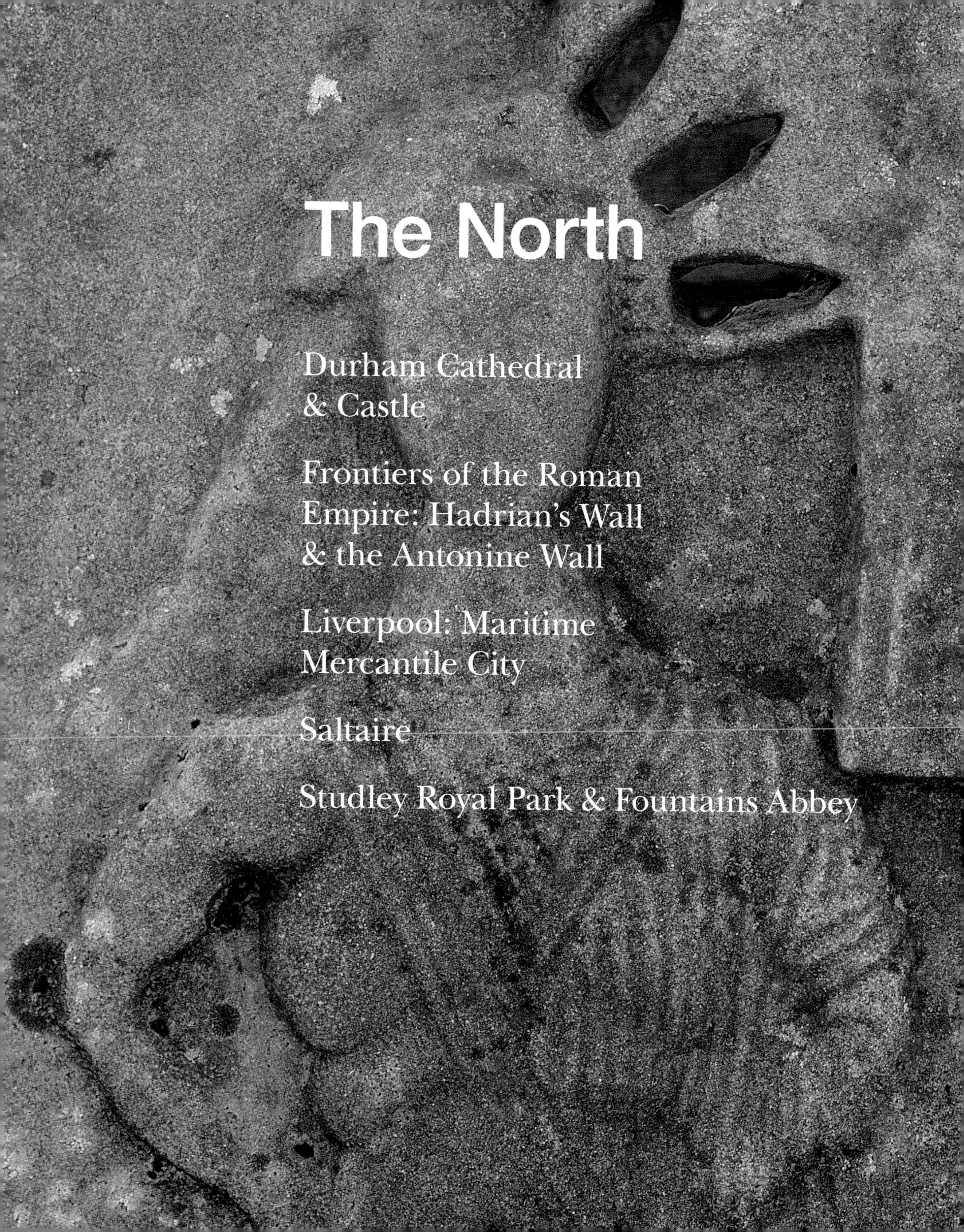

The North

Durham Cathedral
& Castle

Frontiers of the Roman
Empire: Hadrian's Wall
& the Antonine Wall

Liverpool: Maritime
Mercantile City

Saltaire

Studley Royal Park & Fountains Abbey

Durham Cathedral
& Castle

There are two kings in England, namely the Lord King of England, wearing a crown in sign of his regality, and the Lord Bishop of Durham, wearing a mitre in place of a crown, in sign of his regality in the diocese of Durham.
Steward of Anthony Bek, Bishop of Durham (1284–1311)

For centuries, Durham was ruled by the powerful Prince Bishops, who were virtually kings of their county. The Bishop of Durham has always enjoyed the title 'Bishop by Divine Providence', as opposed to all other bishops who are 'Bishops by Divine Right'. However, as the old Saxon kingdom of Northumbria was so far from Westminster, the bishops of Durham enjoyed extraordinary powers, such as the ability to hold their own parliament, raise armies, administer their own laws, appoint sheriffs and justices, levy taxes and customs duties, create fairs and markets, issue charters, salvage shipwrecks, collect revenue from mines, administer forests and even to mint their own coins. Every Bishop of Durham from 1071 to 1836 was a Prince Bishop, except for the first Conqueror-appointed Bishop Walcher, who had been called an Earl Bishop. The last Prince Bishop of Durham was Bishop William Van Mildert (1826–1836), who is credited with the foundation of Durham University.

Grey towers of Durham
Yet well I love thy mixed and massive piles
Half church of God, half castle 'gainst the Scot
And long to roam these venerable aisles
With records stored of deeds long since forgot.
From 'Harold the Dauntless' (1816) by Sir Walter Scott (1771–1832)

Scott's description of Durham Cathedral is well known but, nearly two centuries later, the spectacular view from Prebends Bridge of the cathedral and castle towering above a sweeping horseshoe peninsula in the River Wear continues to amaze and enthral visitors from all over the world. One of the most recent to express his wonder was the American travel writer and celebrated anglophile Bill Bryson, who since 2005 has been Chancellor of Durham University. In 1995, he wrote in his book *Notes from a Small Island*, 'I unhesitatingly gave Durham my vote for best cathedral on planet Earth.'

Durham was inscribed as a cultural World Heritage Site in 1986, in recognition of its place as home to the largest and finest example of Norman architecture in England. The dramatic view of the cathedral and castle perched above the winding river, as extolled by Scott, only serves to enhance its status.

A short history of Durham

The first recorded name of Durham was Dun Holm, derived from Anglo-Saxon and Norse, like so many place names in this part of the world. Its literal meaning is 'hill island' – 'dun' is Saxon for hill, while 'holm' is a Scandinavian word meaning island (see box, left). Dun Holm was called Duresme by the Normans; in Latin it is rendered as Dunelm. The first church on the wooded peninsula was intended as the final resting place of Northumberland's favourite saint, St Cuthbert (see boxes, left and p.136). This small, temporary, wooden church was built from the abundant trees on the site, and is thought to have occupied the site of the present church of St Mary le Bow in Durham. It was eventually replaced by a whitewashed wooden building called the White Church, or Alba Ecclesia, in the centre of the Dun Holm peninsula. The White Church remained in use until 998, when it was replaced by a Saxon minster built of stone.

The cathedral

Renowned as a masterpiece of Romanesque architecture, magnificent Durham Cathedral has been described as 'one of the great architectural experiences of Europe'. It was constructed by Bishops William of St Calais and Rannulph Flambard between 1093 and 1133, and what we see today was largely completed within that astonishingly short period of 40 years. It was the first cathedral in the country to be vaulted in stone, and one of the earliest buildings in Europe to use ribbed vaulting throughout its construction.

As you enter Durham Cathedral by the North Porch, the first impression of the marching, massive cylindrical piers of the nave, with their boldly incised, alternating patterns of diamonds and chevrons, is truly breathtaking. It is like entering a massive forest of stone, yet the overall impression is one of harmonious strength and unity, especially when sunlight floods in from the clerestories above.

There are many architectural highlights to experience during a visit to Durham Cathedral. Perhaps one of the most perfect realizations of the transition between the Romanesque and the Gothic is the delightful Galilee Chapel at the west end, built by Bishop Hugh de Puiset in the 1170s. Here, the massive strength of the piers in the nave is replaced by the lightness and simplicity of Gothic arches, all of which are heavily decorated in zigzag ornamentation. The Venerable Bede (c.672–735), the Jarrow monk known as the 'Father of English History' through his Ecclesiastical History of the English People, is buried in a simple grave here.

The well-travelled remains of St Cuthbert (see box, p.136) are interred behind the high altar in the Early English Chapel of the Nine Altars. Separating the shrine from the altar is the superb Neville Screen, which was installed in 1380 and originally

Left: Durham Cathedral

THE RESTLESS BONES OF ST CUDDY

St Cuthbert (c.634–687), known as St Cuddy, probably travelled further dead than when he was alive. Before his body was finally laid to rest in a shrine at the newly built Durham Cathedral in 1104, the monks of Lindisfarne Priory, fearing Viking invasions, wandered Northumberland for seven years, carrying his bones with them. They were given a resting place for the bones at a church in Chester-le-Street, near Durham, in 883. But, in the late 10th century, a fresh Danish invasion threatened, so the bones were moved again, this time to Ripon. After only a few months at Ripon, poor Cuthbert was once more on the move. His bones were laid in the first wooden church at Durham, where miraculous signs apparently indicated that this was where the saint wished to be buried. A series of churches was built over time to house the relics. The earliest stone church was consecrated in around 999. During William the Conqueror's 'Harrying of the North' in 1069, the bones were moved back to Lindisfarne for safety, but were eventually returned to Durham in 1104. During this final move, the body was found to be perfectly preserved, as was the head of St Oswald, which had been placed with Cuthbert's body for safety.

housed 107 alabaster figures. Sadly, these were removed during the Reformation in the 16th century.

There is a well-appointed shop and museum, which displays relics of St Cuthbert. These include the ornate pectoral cross, which was found around his neck when his body was exhumed, and fragments of his wooden coffin.

The castle

In 1069, the Normans occupied the town that had built up around the Saxon minster. But after William the Conqueror's emissary Robert Cumin was killed in a revolt led by the Earls of Northumberland, William ordered the building of a castle on the same peninsula. Started by Earl Waltheof in around 1072, the castle was built on the classic Norman motte and bailey plan. Little, however, remains of the original Norman building, apart from the chapel, which has been described as 'one of the most powerful expressions of early Norman architecture in the country', and the gallery with its chevron arches in the top storey of the north range of the castle.

Work continued on the castle throughout the Norman period. This included Bishop William Walcher's hall on the site of the present Great Hall, which was built by Bishop Anthony Bek in 1284, and the range of buildings built by Bishop Hugh de Puiset, now occupied by the State Rooms and Norman Gallery.

Durham Castle remained the principal residence of the Prince Bishops of Durham throughout the Middle Ages. Following the creation of the University of Durham in 1832, the castle became one of its first residential colleges. It serves that purpose to this day, with the magnificent Great Hall built by Bishop Bek still used for university graduation ceremonies.

Above: Sunset at Durham Castle
Right: The nave of Durham Cathedral

Frontiers of the Roman Empire: Hadrian's Wall & the Antonine Wall

There is no doubt that this great Roman Wall, from Tyne to Solway, this mighty relic of a mighty people, gains a wonderful hold on the affections of those who follow its course, stirring the imagination and quickening the pulses in a way that could hardly be expected from a mere crumbling ruin.

From *Hadrian's Wall* (1922) by Jessie Mothersole

It's a humbling thought as you stride out along the highest and most spectacular part of the Hadrian's Wall National Trail between Walltown and Chesters that the view has remained unchanged since Roman auxiliary soldiers were garrisoned here nearly 2,000 years ago.

To the north, the 84-mile (135-km) long trail extends across the empty, rain-soaked, lough-spattered wilderness, where a lurking, ever-present threat to the Romans came from the barbarian Caledonians. To the south, it goes as far as the legionary supply fort at Vindolanda (see box, right) and the high fells of the North Pennines. With its steep northern-facing crags and southern slopes bright with wildflowers in summer, there are few landscapes in Britain where the view has hardly changed over two millennia or where you can get such a real, almost tangible, sense of the ancient past.

Hadrian's Wall, still mightily impressive today, was a masterpiece of military engineering, and it remains one of the finest examples of Roman military architecture anywhere in Europe. Built between AD 120 and 128, it ran for 73 miles (117km) across the neck of England, from the Tyne to the Solway. Hadrian's Wall was originally inscribed as a World Heritage Site in 1987, and then extended by UNESCO in 2005 under the international category of Frontiers of the Roman Empire. The 39-mile (63-km) Antonine Wall, built in AD 142 on the orders of Antoninus Pius across the narrowest point of Scotland between Bo'ness on the Firth of Forth and Old Kilpatrick on the Firth of Clyde, was included under the same category in 2008. Built at the behest of the Emperor Hadrian, the Wall was intended to mark the northernmost limit of his empire and also as a barrier against possible invasion by the Caledonians from what we now know as Scotland. Current thinking is that the Wall served a dual purpose – as defence and, perhaps more importantly, as a political border.

Above: An artist's reconstruction of fighting on Hadrian's Wall

If I have to spend the rest of my life working in dirty, wet trenches, I doubt whether I shall ever again experience the shock and excitement I felt at my first glimpse of ink hieroglyphics on tiny scraps of wood.

From *Vindolanda* by archaeologist Robin Birley, recalling his discovery of Roman writing tablets in 1973.

Birley unearthed the tablets from a soaking wet drainage pit at Vindolanda, a mile (1.6km) to the south of Hadrian's Wall. The messages were written in ink with a Roman *stylus* (pen) onto so-called 'leaf' tablets, made of imported spruce or larch. The wooden tablets were preserved because they had been dumped into a wet ditch, where the anaerobic conditions prevented rotting. Vindolanda's unique writing tablets are still being unearthed today, with most being sent to the British Museum in London for restoration and then interpretation. A great deal has been discovered about what everyday life was like for the soldiers and their families stationed at Hadrian's Wall nearly 2,000 years ago. The fragile tablets tell us not only what people ate and drank, but what they wore, and even what they thought of some of their senior colleagues. There is a cook's diary, giving details of who had been to dinner and menus; and requests for woollen socks and underpants – essential for anyone stationed at Hadrian's Wall.

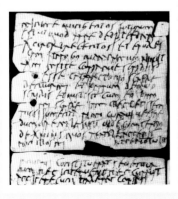

It is amazing to think that it took the force of about 10,000 professional legionaries (not, as is often supposed, British slaves) only eight years to build the Wall, with its series of turrets, milecastles, forts and the vallum. The vallum – an open ditch with embankments set on either side – acted as a sort of political no-man's-land between the Wall and the military road (the modern B6318), which ran parallel to it to the south. Local stone was quarried for the Wall's masonry from nearby Barcombe Hill and also from Limestone Corner, which is actually on the Wall. Here, the vallum was never completed perhaps because of the hardness of the basalt (not, in fact, limestone) rocks. You can still see the marks left by the Roman masons.

A walk along the Wall

Probably the most impressive and certainly the best-known and most heavily visited site on the Wall is Housesteads, the most complete example of a Roman fort in Britain. Originally built between AD 120 and 125, and covering 5 acres, it was occupied throughout the 3rd and 4th centuries by the First Cohort of Tungrians, an 800-strong infantry regiment raised in modern-day Belgium.

The characteristic playing card shape of Roman forts is echoed at Housesteads (or Vercovicium, as it was known), and the north wall is adjacent to the defensive escarpment of the Great Whin Sill ridge (see box). As you walk up to the fort from the well-appointed museum (English Heritage), you pass through the remains of what was once a busy civilian settlement (*vicus*) outside the walls of the fort.

Above: An aerial view of Housesteads Fort
Overleaf: The granary buildings at Housesteads

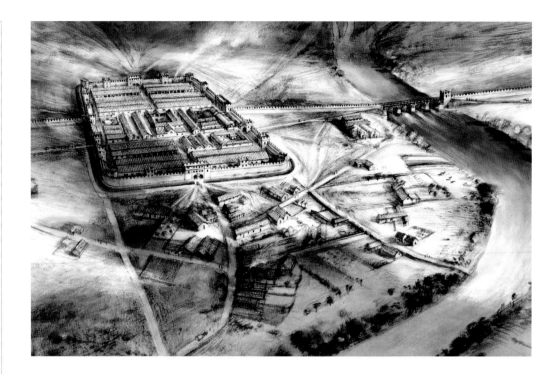

Entering by the south gate, the fort is laid out before you. You can clearly see the foundations of the headquarters building of the garrison, the commanding officer's house, the granaries, the barracks and the hospital. But the foundations that usually attract the most attention are those of the latrine block, which would have had a row of wooden seats over the main sewer channel, fed by water from the adjacent tanks. The smaller channel was used for washing sponges, the Roman equivalent of toilet paper. Unlike Housesteads, the fort at Chesters (*Cilurnum*) in the valley of the River North Tyne near Chollerford was for Roman cavalry, so the stables form an important part of the visible remains. The Second Cavalry Regiment of Asturians (from Spain) were stationed here for an incredible total of 200 years. Chesters was built around AD 213 to protect the bridge that carried the Wall over the North Tyne.

One of the most interesting features of Chesters (English Heritage) is the bathhouse, situated outside the walls of the fort and one of the best-preserved buildings in Roman Britain. The changing rooms (with seven arched niches, possibly for hanging clothes), warm and cold bathing areas (the *tepidarium* and *frigidarium*), steam rooms, hypocaust (underfloor heating) and latrines are all clearly visible. Reconstructions in the excellent, recently renovated museum originally set up by the local landowning Clayton family over a century ago show that, as at Housesteads, the Chesters fort also had a thriving civilian settlement.

The Roman town of Corbridge (*Corstopitum*) was probably occupied longer than any other site along Hadrian's Wall. The first fort was established here around AD 80, and occupation continued, with just one break, well into the 160s. The strategic

Left: Columns outside the granary buildings at *Corstopitum* (Corbridge)
Above: A reconstructed aerial view of Chesters fort by artist Alan Sorrell

importance of Corbridge sprang from its position at the junction of the Roman roads of Stanegate, which ran west to Carlisle, and Dere Street, leading north towards Scotland and south to London. It also controlled the lowest crossing point of the River Tyne.

Originally built by Julius Agricola during his campaigns against the Caledonians, Corbridge fort eventually became the arsenal and ordnance depot for the entire eastern part of the frontier. The town outside the fort extended over 30 acres and was one of the most populous and important settlements along the Wall.

The existing remains at Corbridge (in the care of English Heritage) include the granaries, which fed the troops; a large fountain, from which came the famous carving known as the 'Corbridge Lion'; the courtyard buildings; temples; an underground strongroom; and the headquarters of the garrison. There is another excellent museum, with reconstructions of how the site once looked, along with exhibits of artefacts found there.

But for a real taste of how the legionaries and auxiliaries lived when posted to the Wall, visit the fascinating reconstructions that have been carried out at the forts at South Shields (*Arbeia*) and Wallsend (*Segedunum*) located at the easternmost extremity of the Wall.

The first major reconstruction on the site, carried out in 1986, was the imposing west gateway of the South Shields fort (an important supply base for other forts along the Wall), built to its original height and magnificence. Since then, the Arbeia Society, a group of local enthusiasts, has reconstructed in painstaking detail half of the Roman commanding officer's house and the soldiers' barracks.

The officer's house shows how, in the 4th century, the officer classes continued to enjoy Mediterranean-style luxury living, despite being posted to the northernmost extremity of the Roman Empire. Perhaps the most striking feature of the Arbeia reconstructions is the use of bright colours in the paintwork and in the furnishing of some of the rooms. This brings the past vividly to life in a way that the minimal stone foundations of most of the other sites along the Wall cannot.

The main feature at the Wallsend site is the futuristic observation tower. This was constructed to overlook the site of the mixed infantry and cavalry fort that had been built in the earliest days of the Wall under the orders of Hadrian. The view from the tower shows clearly the shape and outline of the fort, and extends to the tower blocks of Newcastle and the River Tyne.

Right: Hadrian's Wall seen from
Highshield Crags

At the Wallsend fort, the main reconstructed feature is the baths, situated on a former industrial wasteland. Although baths have not yet been discovered on this site, the red-tiled, white-painted building is based faithfully on the baths excavated at the Chesters fort (see page 143). It is a real revelation to see how much bigger and more impressive the buildings look when walls and a roof are added.

Other important sites along Hadrian's Wall worth a visit include Carrawburgh (*Brocolitia*) fort at its northernmost point, with its impressive temple to the goddess Mithras; Birdoswald fort, set spectacularly on a high promontory and overlooking the wooded meanders of the River Irthing near Bewcastle; and the town of Maryport, on the Solway Firth at the western end of the Wall. Here, a former Victorian naval battery has been converted into the Senhouse Museum, and there is a reconstructed timber tower based on a design taken from Trajan's Column in Rome.

The Antonine Wall

The remains of the Antonine Wall, a turf rampart on a stone foundation stretching across central Scotland, are much less evident than those of Hadrian's Wall to the south. Most of the Wall and its associated fortifications, between Bo'ness on the Firth of Forth and Old Kilpatrick on the River Clyde, have been destroyed, but there are still some faint traces. The most visible remains are at Kinneil, at the eastern end of the Wall near Bo'ness, and at Barr Hill, near Twechar. The remains of the ditch are most evident between Twechar and Croy.

The Antonine Wall was built by Emperor Antoninus Pius over a period of 12 years from AD 142 as the northernmost frontier of the Roman Empire, after pressure from the native Caledonians had caused him to send troops further north. It was about 3m (10ft) high and 4.5m (15ft) wide. There was a broad ditch dug in front as part of the defences, with the fill from the ditch forming a low mound to the north. The Wall was protected by 16 forts, with a number of fortlets between them. Troop movements were facilitated by a road linking the forts known as the Military Way.

The Wall was abandoned after only 20 years, and the garrisons were relocated back to Hadrian's Wall. In AD 208, Emperor Septimius Severus re-established legions at the Wall and ordered repairs to be made – this is the reason why it is sometimes referred to as the Severan Wall. However, the occupation ended only a few years later, and the Wall was never fortified again.

Left: Trees covering the ramparts of the Antonine Wall

Liverpool: Maritime Mercantile City

Nothing gives one so vivid an idea of the vast commerce of the country as these docks, quays and immense warehouses, piled and cumbered with hides and merchandises of all kinds from all corners of the world.

Diarist Rev. Francis Kilvert (1840–1879), describing the Liverpool docks in 1872

Liverpool's famous Pier Head on the River Mersey is dominated by the trio of landmark buildings dubbed the Three Graces. On the site of the former George's Dock, the stately Royal Liver, Cunard and Port of Liverpool Buildings are always a welcome sight to returning Liverpudlians, and they epitomize the unique maritime history of the city and the former glory of the British Empire.

The award of World Heritage Site status was made in 2004, based on the fact that Liverpool was 'the supreme example of a commercial port at a time of Britain's greatest global influence'. The area's historic significance centres on its involvement in the growth of world trade, mercantile culture, the transatlantic slave trade (see box, p.153) and mass emigration to North America.

For many emigrants, the last they would see of Britain as they sailed out of Liverpool was the Three Graces. In the century between 1830 and 1930, over 9 million people emigrated from the city to new lives in America and Canada. Meanwhile, many thousands of Irish immigrants arrived during the diaspora following the disastrous potato famine in their home country in 1846–7.

The Liverpool World Heritage Site stretches along the waterfront from the Albert Dock, through the Pier Head and up to Stanley Dock. It then continues through the historic commercial districts to the cultural quarter on the St George's Plateau, which is dominated by the classical facade of St George's Hall.

Some notable buildings

The Grade I listed Royal Liver Building, headquarters of the Royal Liver Friendly Society, is probably the best-known building in the city. It was designed by Walter Aubrey Thomas and built between 1908 and 1911. Eight storeys high, it is fronted by two central clock towers, each crowned by the mythical Liver Birds (see box, left). It was the first building made of reinforced concrete in the world.

Next door is the Cunard Building, the former headquarters of the famous Blue Riband Cunard Line shipping company. Also constructed in reinforced concrete, between 1914 and 1916, this Grade II* listed building is said to have been designed to resemble a ship, wider at the back, where it faces The Strand, than the front, which faces the Mersey.

The Grade II* listed Port of Liverpool Building, the third of the Three Graces, is the former home of the Mersey Docks and Harbour Board. It was built in the classical style between 1903 and 1907, and features an 11-bay facade and a large copper-covered central dome.

The Pier Head has been the subject of a number of redevelopment schemes. The ill-fated 'Fourth Grace' project in 2002 started with a competition to design a fourth building for the Pier Head waterfront. The futuristic winning entry, designed by Will Alsop and known as the Cloud, was abandoned in 2004 after fundamental changes to the waterfront plan made it unworkable.

In 2007, work commenced on a new scheme to rehouse the Museum of Liverpool Life in a new Museum of Liverpool. Due to open in 2011 on the Mann Island site at the Pier Head, the museum will demonstrate Liverpool's unique contribution to the world's commerce, maritime trade, industry and music, and will showcase popular culture while tackling social, historical and contemporary issues. Work also commenced in 2007 to build a canal link between the Leeds–Liverpool Canal and the South Docks. Passing the Pier Head and the Three Graces, the 1.6-mile (2.6-km) extension to the existing 127 miles (204km) of canal was officially opened in March 2009 at a cost of £22m.

The brick-red Doric colonnades of the Albert Dock building was opened by its namesake, Prince Albert, in 1846, as much-needed warehouses. It constitutes the

Top left: Depiction of Liverpool from the *Illustrated London News*
Left: Engraving of The Goree Warehouse, c.1830
Overleaf: The Royal Liver, Cunard and Port of Liverpool buildings

largest collection of Grade I listed buildings in the country. Now tastefully restored, it is home to Tate Liverpool, the Merseyside Maritime and Customs and Excise Museums, and the International Slavery Museum (see box, left), as well as other galleries, restaurants, cafes and high-class shops.

Also on the site at George's Dock is the cathedral-like Mersey Tunnel building, to the east of the Port of Liverpool Building. Opened in 1934, it houses offices and ventilator equipment for the 2-mile (3.2-km) long Queensway Tunnel, which links Liverpool with Birkenhead on the other side of the Mersey.

St George's Hall is reckoned to be one of the finest examples of neoclassical design in the world. It was built between 1841 and 1854 as a concert hall and law court to designs by the architects Harvey Lonsdale Elmes and C.R. Cockerell, who was responsible for the interiors. This Grade I listed building is 51m (169ft) long and 22m (74ft) wide, with the largest tunnel-vaulted ceiling in Europe. The impressive ceiling is supported on massive red granite columns, featuring figures portraying those qualities to which Victorian Liverpool aspired – namely art, science, fortitude and justice. Today, it is used mainly as a concert and exhibition hall.

In addition to Cockerell's incredibly ornate gold-leaf interior details and Elmes's classical exterior porticoes, St George's Hall also houses a unique and priceless mosaic floor made up of 30,000 Minton porcelain tiles. When the floor was uncovered to mark the hall's centenary in 1954, more than 100,000 Liverpudlians queued to see it. The hall is also home to an historic Willis concert organ. Its 7,000 pipes make it second only in size to the organ in London's Royal Albert Hall.

Just across Lime Street from St George's Hall is Liverpool's classic Lime Street Station, built between 1867 and 1879 as the terminus of the Liverpool and Manchester Railway. Its soaring roof span, which measures a staggering 61m (200ft), was the largest in the world at the time.

Behind St George's Hall in William Brown Street is the Walker Art Gallery, home to one of the finest collections of fine and decorative art in Europe. It was built between 1874 and 1877, funded by Sir Andrew Barclay Walker, a city brewer, alderman and former lord mayor. The Walker's collection is particularly rich in European old masters and Pre-Raphaelite paintings.

Left: Statue of Benjamin Disraeli in front of the Corinthian columns of St George's Hall

Saltaire

Titus Salt was born in Morley, near Leeds. His father, Daniel, was a successful local mill-owner. After working for two years as a wool-stapler in Wakefield, Titus became his father's partner in the family woollen mill business. He unsuccessfully tried to get other Bradford spinners interested in working with the more easily available Russian donskoi wool, which his firm used to make worsted, so he set up as a spinner and manufacturer himself. He married his wife Caroline in 1830, and the couple had 11 children.

By 1833, Salt had taken over the running of the family business and within 20 years he had become the largest employer in Bradford. In 1851, Salt decided to build a large mill outside Bradford in order to consolidate his textile manufacturing in one place. The mill at Saltaire opened on his 50th birthday in 1853.

From Peru, he has brought the alpaca,
From Asia's plains the mohair;
With skill has wrought both into beauty,
Prized much by the wealthy and fair,
He has Velvets, and Camlets, and Lustres;
With them there is none can compare;
Then off with your bonnets,
And hurrah for the Lord of Saltaire.
19th-century popular song about Titus Salt, founder of Saltaire

Times were tough in the British textile trade in the 1830s. Cotton imports had dried up during the American Civil War, with the Republican states blockading the Southern ports, and an urgent search was on for alternative sources of fibre. In 1836, 33-year-old Titus Salt (see box, left), a partner in his father's Bradford woollen mill, was inspecting some imported fibres in the Liverpool warehouse of Hegan & Co, when he came upon 300 neglected bales of Peruvian alpaca wool. The alpaca is a South American member of the camel family. Its fleece, which is usually clipped every two years, is very long and lustrous. That momentous chance discovery was to make Salt's fortune and eventually create the famous World Heritage Site model industrial village of Saltaire, which was inscribed by UNESCO in 2001. A dramatized account of the fateful event, written by Charles Dickens in his weekly journal *Household Words*, appeared in 1852:

One day, a plain business-looking young man, with an intelligent face and a quiet, reserved manner, was walking alone through those same warehouses at Liverpool, when his eye fell upon some of the superannuated horse-hair projecting from one of the ugly dirty bales…
Our friend took it up, looked at it, felt it, smelt it, rubbed it, pulled it about; in fact, he did all but taste it, and he would have done that if it had suited his purpose, for he was 'Yorkshire'.

Salt took some alpaca wool samples away with him to try them out – Dickens claimed they underwent 'some excruciating private tortures' – then returned to Liverpool and bought the whole consignment. Salt's friends and his father, who called the alpaca 'nasty stuff', tried their best to discourage him from using it. But Salt had made up his mind. As he told his good friend John Hammond: 'Well John, I am going into this alpaca affair right and left, and I'll either make myself a man or a mouse.'

Salt was not the first to try working with alpaca wool, but he was the first successful creator of the lustrous and fashionable cloth that took its name. It was said to give a textile the quality of silk for the price of wool, and even Queen Victoria started to wear alpaca dresses. The cloth subsequently became very fashionable and, along with angora and Russian donskoi wool, a coarse wool generally used for carpets, it made Titus Salt a very rich man.

A tour of Saltaire

When setting up his first mill in 1851, Salt decided he wanted to escape from the grossly polluted and overcrowded conditions that existed at the time in Bradford. The Bradford Canal was a stinking open sewer, and the average life expectancy in the city in the 1840s was just over 20 years, although many children died under the age of five.

Salt decided on a site with good communications, close to the Leeds–Liverpool Canal and the Midland Railway, on the River Aire, about 4 miles (6.4km) from Bradford. His first great Salt's Mill was built in warm yellow sandstone in an Italianate style by local architects Henry Lockwood and William and Richard Mawson. Work started in 1851 and the mill opened on Salt's 50th birthday, in 1853. The mayor of Bradford, Samuel Smith, said Salt had built a 'palace of industry almost equal to the palaces of the Caesars'.

Salt's Mill, which employed about 3,000 workers and housed 1,200 looms, produced an astonishing 30,000 yards (27m) of cloth a day. It boasted many innovative features, such as improved smoke burners, and flues to remove dust and dirt. In addition, the heaviest machinery was confined to the lower levels to suppress the noise. A tunnel led from the mill yard to the Dining Hall, where food was sold at a set price – for example, a good plate of meat and potato pie cost 2d (1p) – and 600 breakfasts and 700 dinners were served every day.

The New Mill to the north of the original mill was built by Salt in 1868 as a spinning mill and dyeworks. Worried that the chimney might spoil the view down Victoria Road, Salt decorated it like the campanile of the church of Santa Maria Gloriosa dei Frari in Venice.

Part of the first Salt's Mill is open to the public today as a cultural centre, shopping outlet and restaurant. The 1853 Gallery houses a huge collection of works by Bradford-born artist David Hockney (see box). These developments followed the purchase of the mill by Jonathan Silver in 1987. In addition to creating an efficient business, Salt's objective, like that of Robert Owen at New Lanark (see p.178–85) and Hill, Hopkins and Pratt at Blaenavon (see p.110), was also philanthropic: he wanted to provide healthier

Top: Statue of Titus Salt
Above: Entrance to the Titus Salt hospital
Overleaf: Salt's mill dominates the town and overlooks the terraced workers' houses

living conditions and a better working environment for his workers. Over the next 20 years, he built more than 775 houses in 22 streets (each named after his children and his architects) for his employees to live in, as well as shops and a 750-roll school. He also provided clean drinking water, bath houses and a nine-bed hospital on Saltaire Road.

Brought up in a Congregationalist household, Salt remained a deeply religious man throughout his life, and the beautiful Congregational (now United Reformed) Church was an important feature of his new model village. Designed by Mawson and Lockwood, the circular Corinthian-columned church was built between 1858 and 1859 for £16,000. It is said that Lady Caroline Salt ordered the gallery to be built so she could sit apart from the workers, while her husband always sat down below with them. The Carrara marble statue of Salt in the church porch was presented to him by his workers in 1856.

Salt also built 45 almshouses around Alexandra Square, a town hall, library, the previously mentioned school and various other municipal buildings, all of which are centred around Victoria Square. Four carved sandstone lions stand at its corners, but it is a myth that the lions were originally destined for London's Trafalgar Square. The Saltaire Institute on Victoria Road, with its baroque entrance and tower, originally housed a lecture theatre that seated 800 people.

Roberts Park, originally called Salt's Park, or Saltaire Park, was also created by Salt as part of his plan to ensure his workers enjoyed a healthy environment with recreational opportunities. In 1903, James Roberts, then owner of the mill, celebrated the centenary of Salt's birth by the erection in the park of a fine statue of the founder of this unique experiment in social welfare.

Left: The dome of the United Reform Church in Saltaire
Above right: Salt's Mill by David Hockney, painted in oils on two canvases

Studley Royal Park & Fountains Abbey

On a bleak midwinter day in 1132, Archbishop Thurstan of York brought a group of 13 exiled Benedictine monks from St Mary's Abbey in York to Herleshowe Wood in the wild and uninhabited valley of the River Skell, near Ripon, to establish a new monastery.

It was, according to later chronicles, 'a place remote from all the world… a wild and inhospitable place, more fitting to be the lair of wild beasts than of men'. Initially, the monks had nowhere to shelter except under the outcropping sandstone crags in the valley, then under a great elm tree, which apparently lived on until the 18th century. The monks' exile had followed a bitter dispute at St Mary's Abbey, where they had been unsuccessful in their attempts to return to the spartan, early 6th-century Rule of St Benedict, as exemplified by the Cistercian order (see box, left). They were then taken under the protection of Archbishop Thurstan, who provided them with the site for their first wooden monastery in the valley of the River Skell. Despite its remoteness, which appealed to the Cistercians whose stated ambition was 'a marvellous freedom from the tumult of the world', it had all the requirements for the creation of a monastery. There was shelter from the harsh northern weather, stone and wood for building, and an essential supply of running water.

From these humble and unpromising beginnings grew the great Cistercian abbey of Fountains, one of the largest foundations of the order and one of the most important and powerful monastic sites in the whole of Europe. Together with the Aislabie family's beautiful 18th-century landscaped gardens in the Studley Royal estate, it became one of the first British World Heritage Sites in 1986.

A Tour of the Abbey

The most striking feature of Fountains Abbey, as you approach it from the award-winning National Trust Visitor Centre on the hillside above, is the Bell Tower. Built by Abbot Marmaduke Huby, this magnificent 52-m (170-ft) high tower was added to the end of the north transept in the late 15th century.

The tower was obviously designed to impress, rising from a deep moulded plinth and supported by massive angle buttresses. Originally decorated by statues of angels, abbots and saints and the initials of Huby himself, the only ornamentation still just about visible is the Latin text under the parapet, which was Huby's personal motto:

Soli Deo Honor et Gloria (Only to God honour and glory). Although the bells, floors and roof of the four-storeyed building are long gone, the tower remains one of the finest in the north of England, showing its position as Huby's 'golden and unbreakable column in his zeal for the order'.

Our tour of the abbey begins at the rather austere West Front, built in about 1160, which faces you across the abbey green. The stones for this massive building were hewn from the adjacent sandstone outcrops along the north side of the valley. Entering by the great west door, you are immediately faced with a wonderful uninterrupted vista towards the east end, framed by the massive Norman pillars of the Nave and the north and south aisles.

The South Transept is thought to be the site of the original wooden church built in 1133, and is the oldest part of the abbey. The beautiful Early English Presbytery and Chapel of the Nine Altars, which is similar to Durham's (see p.134-7), were built in the early part of the 13th century and adorned with shafts of local Nidderdale 'marble'. Note the angel on the apex of one arch in the chapel, inserted after settlement damage, and a corresponding Green Man on the outside wall (see box, p.165).

The Cloisters were the nerve centre of the abbey, used by the monks for meditation and exercise. Among the many rooms leading off the cloisters is the Chapter House, the administrative centre of the abbey, so-called because this was where a chapter of the Rule of St Benedict was read daily. In the Warming Room, you can still see the huge fireplace where a roaring fire provided much-needed warmth. Above this, the external day staircase rose to the monks' dormitory and the muniments room, where important documents were kept.

Above: Fountains Abbey
Overleaf: Studley Royal Estate and Fountains Abbey

A doorway on the west side of the cloister leads to the Cellarium and Lay Brothers' Refectory in the magnificent west range. The sight of the beautiful arches springing up from the dirt floor to the incredible vaulted ceiling down the 90-m (300-ft) length of the cellarium is unforgettable. This is where the lay brothers (*conversi*) ate and socialized, but they would not have enjoyed this view – in the 12th century, the area would have been partitioned off when the building was used for storage purposes. Today, the only inhabitants are protected bats, which live in the nooks and crannies of the ceiling. Also in the grounds is the Abbey Mill, the only 12th-century Cistercian corn mill in Britain and one of only a few surviving in Europe. It was built originally as a huge watermill and granary, but in its time it has also been a sawmill, a stone mason's workshop and even a generating station for electricity.

The elegant Jacobean facade of Fountains Hall was built by Sir Stephen Proctor between 1598 and 1604, partly using stone from the abbey ruins. Three rooms are open to the public: the Stone Hall with its minstrels' gallery, the Arkell room, used as exhibition space, and the Reading Room. The rest of the hall is used by the National Trust as holiday apartments.

The Studley Royal Water Gardens

John Aislabie inherited the Studley Royal estate in 1699 through his mother's family. Socially and politically ambitious, he had became the Tory Member of Parliament for Ripon in 1695, and in 1718, helped by a timely change in his political allegiance to the Whig party, rose to the dizzy heights of Chancellor of the Exchequer. However, disaster soon followed in 1720, when he was expelled from Parliament and disqualified from public office for his part in the South Sea Bubble, the world's first and, arguably, greatest financial scandal.

Aislabie returned to Yorkshire and devoted himself to creating what has been described as the best English water garden to have survived from the early 18th century. After his death in 1742, his son William, also MP for Ripon, extended his father's work by purchasing the abbey ruins. He enlarged the landscaped gardens in the picturesque Romantic style, perhaps as a result of his Grand Tour of Italy in 1720. The 150-acre Water Gardens, with its formal, geometrical designs and wonderful vistas, was inspired by the work of the great French landscape gardeners but seems to have been entirely John Aislabie's personal vision. The only professional advice he appears to have received was from the distinguished Palladian architect Colen Campbell, who probably designed the Banqueting House. Originally envisaged as an orangery, this was later embellished, deliberately rusticated and fitted out as a banqueting house with some fine wood carving inside by Richard Fisher of York.

Left: Sunshine and shadows in the aisles of Fountains Abbey

Probably one of the most photographed views in the Water Gardens is across the still, circular waters of the Moon Pond to the classical Temple of Piety. This was one of the last features added by John Aislabie, in 1729–30, and was originally dedicated to Hercules. Designed as a cool garden house on the shady, wooded side of the valley, it is a perfect example of neoclassicism. After the death of his father in 1742, William Aislabie redesigned the building as a symbol of filial piety.

Classical statues punctuate the whole of the Water Gardens, and the Moon Pond, with its flanking crescent basins, provides the setting for the lead statues of Bacchus, Neptune and Galen. Strangely, the only stone statue in the garden depicts Hercules and Antaeus, alongside the Formal Canal.

Follies were very popular features in Georgian gardens. Examples at Studley include the pinnacled gothic Octagon Tower on a high rocky outcrop reached through the twisting Serpentine Tunnel, and the Temple of Fame, a rotunda with a ring of wooden columns painted to look like stone. There are wonderful views across the gardens from this high path, but perhaps the finest view in the Studley Royal gardens is the so-called Surprise View from Anne Boleyn's Seat at the end of the High Ride path.

Approached from behind, through the trees, there is no warning of what will be revealed from the shelter, which was named after a previously decapitated statue of Henry VIII's second wife. The abbey suddenly appears in all its ruined glory far below in the valley, rising serenely from the banks of the River Skell. The view is as impressive today as it was when William Aislabie envisaged it over two centuries ago.

A stunning, although often overlooked, feature of the 400-acre Deer Park, with its 350-strong herd of red and Sika deer, is the church of St Mary the Virgin. This is an unheralded masterpiece of High Victorian religious Gothic architecture, designed by William Burges for the 1st Marquess of Ripon and built between 1871 and 1879. The relatively restrained Early English-style exterior gives no clue to the richly decorated and vividly coloured inside, which owes much to Burges's interest in medieval art and Christian symbolism, where light and colour are used to truly dramatic effect.

The chancel and sanctuary are flamboyantly decorated with carved angels and lions of Judah set against rich red and gold walls and a riot of stained glass. The circular sanctuary roof over the altar is a golden vision of heaven, with angels playing different musical instruments. Multicoloured parrots perch above the choir stalls, some of them seeming to peck away at the gold-leaf tracery surrounding them. There could not be a more complete contrast with the austere simplicity of the ruined Cistercian abbey in the valley below.

Right: This lead statue of Bacchus stands at the edge of one of the crescent pools

Scotland & Northern Ireland

Old & New Edinburgh

New Lanark

Neolithic Orkney

St Kilda

Giant's Causeway

Old & New Edinburgh

Recently voted the most desirable UK city in which to live, Edinburgh must also be the one with the most nicknames. Affectionately known as 'Auld Reekie' in recognition of its former notoriously smoky and polluted atmosphere, Edinburgh is also often referred to as the 'Athens of the North'.

The city earned this name because of its many fine classical buildings, galleries and museums, as well as the various cultural events that take place here, notably the international Edinburgh Festival, which is held every summer between July and September. It was also known by the Latin names of *Aneda* or *Edina*, and the adjectival *Edinensis* is still to be found inscribed on many public buildings.

Edinburgh has also been called Dunedin. This was derived from the Gaelic *Dùn Èideann*, or 'the fort of Eidin', an Iron Age hillfort sited on the crag where the castle now stands. Interestingly, the city of Dunedin in New Zealand's South Island was originally called New Edinburgh by its Scottish settlers. The great Edinburgh novelist Sir Walter Scott, most famous for his book *Waverley*, referred to the city as the 'Empress of the North', while another novelist son of Auld Reekie, Robert Louis Stevenson, emphatically claimed: 'Edinburgh is what Paris ought to be.'

The World Heritage Site lies at the heart of the city, combining the medieval Old Town and the Georgian New Town, along with the city's award-winning modern architecture. It was inscribed by UNESCO in 1995 in recognition of the unique character of its distinctively different, yet always harmonious, architectural and cultural riches.

A tour of the city

Edinburgh was founded on its volcanic past. An unimaginable 350 million years ago, a huge volcano centred on the 251-m (823-ft) high craggy outcrop of Arthur's Seat, now in the surprisingly wild Holyrood Park, was spewing out quantities of liquid magma and ash. A basalt sill (magma thrust up between earlier layers of rock) gave us the sheer cliffs of Salisbury Crags overlooking the city centre, while a subsidiary volcanic vent gave us the crag on which Edinburgh Castle now stands.

Lording it over the city from its volcanic plug, Edinburgh Castle is Scotland's number one visitor attraction, with outstanding views across 'Auld Reekie' and as far as the Forth bridges to the west on a clear day. Here you can view the Scottish Crown Jewels – known as the 'Honours of Scotland' – and the Stone of Scone in the Crown Room;

the birth chamber in the King's Lodging where James VI of Scotland (James I of England) was born; and the Great Hall, the first home of the Scottish Parliament (see box, p.176).

But one of the most touching and ancient buildings is tiny St Margaret's Chapel, built by David I in the 12th century. There are also two military museums and the Scottish National War Memorial. The most recent addition is the prisoners-of-war experience in the Queen Anne Building.

Beneath the castle walls, the Royal Mile winds through the oldest parts of Edinburgh down to Holyroodhouse. The usually cynical 18th-century journalist Daniel Defoe claimed that the Mile was 'the largest, longest, finest street in the world'. Along its length you will find St Giles' Cathedral, which dates from the 12th century and became a cathedral in 1633; Tolbooth Kirk, built in 1844 by James Gillespie Graham and Augustus Pugin for the General Assembly of the Church of Scotland; Gladstone's Land, a typical 17th-century, six-storey tenement now reconstructed and owned by the National Trust for Scotland; and John Knox's House, possibly the oldest dwelling house in the city, dating from 1490 and once the home of the great religious reformer in the 16th century.

The Palace of Holyroodhouse is the Queen's official residence in Scotland, and home to centuries of fascinating history. You can visit the Royal Apartments, the Throne

Above right: Edinburgh Castle and Princes Street Gardens
Overleaf: Edinburgh at night, seen from Calton Hill

Room and the Gallery, where there are over 80 portraits of Scottish monarchs. Alongside is the recently opened Queen's Gallery, Scotland's first permanent exhibition space for the Royal Collections. The Palace is perhaps best known as the home of Mary, Queen of Scots, and as the setting for the most dramatic episodes in her reign, culminating in the murder of her secretary David Rizzio in 1566.

The neoclassical New Town of Edinburgh, the brainchild of Lord Provost George Drummond, has been described as one of the finest examples of planned 18th-century architecture in the world. Highlights include The Assembly Rooms in George Street, designed by John and David Henderson to echo those of Bath and opened in 1787; and Robert Adam's 1774 imposing 1774 Register House, one of the first major government buildings to be constructed in Britain, which houses the Scottish National Archives. The facade of Register House on North Bridge culminates a particularly fine and iconic vista of the city.

Perhaps the most famous shopping street in Edinburgh is Princes Street, which runs parallel to George Street and Queen Street, with their elegant Georgian houses. William Henry Playfair's temple-like National Gallery of Scotland, the grand exterior of the Royal Scottish Academy on The Mound, and the Gothic fantasy of George Meikle Kemp's Monument to Sir Walter Scott, built on the site of the drained former Nor'Loch and backing onto the Princes Street Gardens, are the principal features of the area around Princes Street.

Left: Smart shops and eating places on Victoria Street
Above right: Charles II statue and St Giles Cathedral

SKATING AROUND CONTROVERSY

We don't want to forget that the Scottish Parliament will be in Edinburgh, but will belong to Scotland, to the Scottish land. The Parliament should be able to reflect the land it represents. The building should arise from the sloping base of Arthur's Seat and arrive into the city almost surging out of the rock.
Enric Miralles, architect of the Scottish Parliament building, 1999

The most controversial modern building within the Edinburgh World Heritage Site is the revolutionary Scottish Parliament building at Holyrood, opened by the Queen in 2004. Politicians, the media and the public all criticized the building's location, architect, design and construction. Although scheduled to open in 2001, it did not do so until 2004, at an estimated final cost of £414m, which was many times higher than the original estimates of between £10m and £40m, a fact that prompted a major public inquiry.

Despite all these criticisms and the mixed public reaction, the building was welcomed by architectural academics and critics, and it won many awards, including the prestigious 2005 Stirling Prize. The architect and critic Charles Jencks described it as 'a tour de force of arts and crafts and quality without parallel in the last 100 years of British architecture'.

The building's Spanish architect, Enric Miralles, who died shortly before its opening, claimed to have taken his inspiration from things as diverse as the flower paintings of Glasgow's Charles Rennie Macintosh, Edwin Lutyens's upturned herring boat sheds on Lindisfarne, and the iconic late 18th-century Scottish painting by Sir Henry Raeburn of *The Reverend Robert Walker Skating on Duddingston Loch below Arthur's Seat*, a picture better known as *The Skating Minister*. Miralles is said to have arrived at the first design meeting carrying a bunch of twigs and leaves. Throwing them onto the table, he declared: 'This is the Scottish Parliament!' He said he wanted the building to reflect a dialogue between the landscape and the act of people debating, making it fit into the landscape 'in the form of a gathering situation: an amphitheatre, coming out from Arthur's Seat'. The end result is a flowing, organic collection of low-lying buildings intended to allow views of, and to blend in with, the surrounding rugged scenery of Arthur's Seat and Salisbury Crags, symbolizing the connection between nature and the Scottish people.

The building has many features relating to nature and the land, from the leaf-shaped motifs of the roof in the Garden Lobby to the windows of the Public Gallery, which look out over the landscaped grounds towards Holyrood Park, and the wild scenery of Salisbury Crags and Arthur's Seat. Inside the buildings, the connection to the land is reinforced by the use of Scottish rock such as gneiss and granite in the floors and walls, and oak and sycamore in the furniture. The series of so-called timber and granite 'trigger panels' over the windows on the north side of the building facing Canongate have been interpreted in a number of different ways. Some say they represent anvils, hairdryers, guns, question marks, even a hammer and sickle. Miralles's widow claimed that the design was simply that of a curtain pulled back from a window, while her late husband once said that he wanted the profile to evoke that icon of Scottish culture, the painting of Reverend Walker skating.

Above: A detail of the new Scottish Parliament Building
Right: Princes Street and St Mary's Cathedral seen from Calton Hill

New Lanark

'Eight hours' daily labour is enough for any human being, and under proper arrangements sufficient to afford an ample supply of food, raiment and shelter, or the necessaries and comforts of life, and for the remainder of his time, every person is entitled to education, recreation and sleep.'

Robert Owen, social reformer, 1833

Robert Owen's founding maxim for his Society for Promoting National Regeneration was the basis for his revolutionary experiment in social welfare and the foundation of a Utopian industrial society in the village of New Lanark, on the banks of the Clyde, southeast of Glasgow. The experiment attracted the attention of other social reformers, presidents, politicians and statesmen from all over the world, including Nicholas, the future tsar of Russia, and James Monroe, the US president. It also provided the touchstone for the co-operative movement, a scheme for sharing profits among employees. This was first successfully adopted in 1844 by the Rochdale Pioneers, a group of weavers and other artisans at the centre of England's textile industry. The idea of a co-operative system came to Owen as a result of the truck system. In the early years of the Industrial Revolution, many mill owners paid their workers in part or totally with tokens. These had no value outside the mill owner's so-called 'truck shops', in which poor-quality goods were sold at top prices. A series

of 'Truck Acts' passed by Parliament between 1831 and 1887 eventually put an end to this practice. Owen, who part-owned a mill in New Lanark, refused to operate the truck system. Instead, he opened a store where goods of sound quality could be bought at little more than wholesale cost, and he also placed the sale of alcohol under strict supervision. He then passed the savings from the bulk purchasing of goods on to his workers. As well as being the basis for the co-operative movement, these principles were also behind the first British trade unions, which Owen helped found. In addition, Owen was the progenitor of infant childcare in Britain, and an early proponent of employment training, social inclusion and the rights of women.

Many of these ideas first expressed by Robert Owen remain just as relevant and topical today. It was the international influence of his campaign for a better and fairer society that was one of the major criteria for New Lanark being assessed by UNESCO as worthy of World Heritage Status, for eventual inscription in 2000.

Today, New Lanark remains an exceptional example of a purpose-built, 18th-century mill village, set in a beautiful landscape near the Falls of Clyde, between Glasgow and Edinburgh. The cotton mills were in operation from 1786 to 1968, and, at the turn of the 19th century, they constituted one of the largest groups of mills in the world, employing 2,000 people, including many children from the age of six upwards.

By the late 1960s, though, New Lanark was in decline and many of the buildings were under threat of demolition. The New Lanark Conservation Trust was set up in 1974 to conserve and restore many of the historic buildings in the village. Today, New Lanark is still a living and working community, with a resident population of around 200 and attracting about 400,000 visitors a year.

The mills today

A visit to the New Lanark World Heritage Site, with its towering mill buildings crammed into a narrow, almost claustrophobic valley, will transport you back to the days when Richard Owen and his radical ideas transformed the lives of his workers and their families, setting the blueprint for social reform throughout the world.

The best place to start your visit is at the Visitor Centre, which is housed in three of the village's red sandstone buildings. You enter via Owen's grandly named Institute for the Formation of Character, one of the first infant schools in the world, which began operation in the 1820s. A classroom complete with slates and desks has been lovingly re-created. You can join a time-traveller from the future in the audio-visual theatre, who shows you the place of New Lanark in world history, highlighting the issues that were important to Robert Owen and which are still relevant today, nearly two centuries later. The ghost of the little mill girl Annie McLeod tells the story of

Far left: Robert Owen
Left: New Harmony, Indiana, Owen's failed Utopia
Overleaf: The Spinning Mill's New Buildings on the banks of the River Clyde

NEW LANARK 179

her life in New Lanark in the 1820s in the Annie McLeod Experience Ride. In the adjoining Engine House, there is a restored Petrie steam engine.

Other attractions in the village include two re-created tenements, known as the Millworkers' House, in a block now restored chiefly for modern accommodation. Here you can see how Owen's workers lived, including their sleeping, eating and washing arrangements. Prominent in the Village Square is the Village Store, the forerunner of all our modern Co-op supermarkets, which Owen built to give his workers good-quality produce and goods at reasonable prices.

The New Lanark Mill Hotel is an award-winning, 38-bedroomed conversion from the original 18th-century cotton mill, with fantastic views across the surrounding conservation area and River Clyde. Also incorporated in the mill buildings are a coffee shop, gift shop and Owen's warehouse. Owen himself lived with his family at the modest, gabled Braxfield House, overlooking the gardens in the centre of the community. The house has been restored to how it was when Owen was devising his radical plans for social improvement.

Don't miss the stunning views from the unique 836-sq m (9,000-sq ft) Roof Garden on the top of Mill No. 2, with its spectacular bird's-eye view of the historic village and surrounding scenery. The amazing garden is the largest of its kind in Scotland, with over 70 different plants and shrubs, a central water feature and sculptures, which visitors can enjoy all year round. The innovative design won a Commendation in the Scottish Design Awards in 2009.

The decision to build a garden on the roof of the mill was influenced strongly by the views of Owen. He believed in the importance of the environment and natural history, and argued that a pleasant environment was essential for happy, healthy communities. In 1817, he wrote of his workers: 'They will be surrounded by gardens, have abundance of space in all directions to keep the air healthy and pleasant: they will have walks and plantations before them, and well cultivated grounds, kept in good order, as far as the eye can reach.'

Owen would undoubtedly be delighted by the adjacent Falls of Clyde Wildlife Reserve. Run by the Scottish Wildlife Trust, it is home to over 100 species of birds, including the rare peregrine falcon. An easy 25-minute walk south from New Lanark through mixed and ancient woodland will take you to the 28-m (92-ft) high waterfall at Corra Linn, which was the inspiration for paintings by J M W Turner and poems by William Wordsworth. The reserve is part of the Clyde Valley Woodlands National Nature Reserve, a Site of Special Scientific Interest, a Special Area for Conservation, as well as part of the World Heritage Site.

Left: 'Hares' by Laura Antebi in the New Lanark Roof Garden, designed by Viridarium

Heart of Neolithic Orkney

We tend to regard graffiti as a modern phenomenon. However, in 1861, when the archaeologist James Farrer excavated the 5,000-year-old Neolithic passage grave of Maes Howe on Mainland in the Orkneys, he was surprised to discover that he was not the first visitor.

When Farrer realized he was unable to enter the chamber of the grave through the blocked entrance passage, he drove a shaft down from the top of the 11-m (36-ft) high, grass-covered mound. Once inside the central chamber, he found that the walls of the New Stone Age tomb were covered in runic graffiti. These 33 inscriptions form one of the largest and most famous collection of runes (see box, right) known in Europe. According to the *Orkneyinga Saga*, written around AD 1200, one dark winter's night on Orkney over 800 years before, a group of Viking warriors, led by Earl Harald Maddadarson, had sought shelter from a terrible snowstorm in the ancient structure they called *Orkahaugr* (Maes Howe). Once inside, as they waited for the storm to abate, they carved the runic graffiti, along with representations of a dragon, a walrus and a serpent knot, into the smooth stone walls. One of the inscriptions may have explained the Vikings' true purpose. Translated it says: 'Crusaders broke into Maeshowe. Lif the earl's cook carved these runes. To the northwest is a great treasure hidden. It was long ago that a great treasure was hidden here. Happy is he that might find that great treasure. Hakon alone bore treasure from this mound.'

Above: The interior of the Maes Howe chamber shortly after it was re-opened in 1861
Right: Engraved Viking runes on a stone found in Maes Howe

When people first began to communicate through the written word, they had to use simple angular lettering that could be easily scratched with a blade or an axe onto stone or wood. Over time, these rough scratches developed into the more complex writing form now known as runes, which comes from the Old Norse for 'secret writing'.

The earliest runic inscriptions date from around AD 150, and runes were in use in various Germanic languages prior to the adoption of the Latin alphabet after the advent of Christianity. They continued to be used in places like rural Sweden until the early 20th century for specialized purposes, such as decorating runic calendars.

Runes are formed by angular, straight lines, a shape dictated by the materials used to create them. The simplicity of the runic alphabet meant that any messages, like those in the Maes Howe tomb, could be inscribed quite quickly and easily.

Apart from the collection of runes found at Maes Howe, there are about a score of other runic inscriptions in Orkney, including in the stalled cairn of Unstan and on one of the standing stones within the Ring of Brodgar.

When the 12th-century Round Kirk (church) at Orphir was demolished in 1757, a stone was discovered with a runic inscription, which apparently read: 'The church is not good.' The stone may have been reused, however, because during the demolition in 1953 of the 18th-century parish church that stood at the western side of the old Round Kirk, a rune-inscribed stone was found. This stone is now kept in the Orkney Museum in Kirkwall.

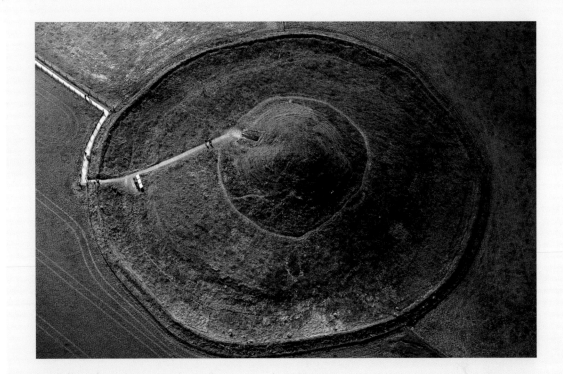

Maes Howe, together with the Neolithic village of Skara Brae, the stone circles of the Ring of Brodgar and the Stones of Stenness make up one of the most remarkable collections of megalithic monuments in Britain, and form the centrepiece of the Heart of Orkney World Heritage Site, which was inscribed in 1999.

Maes Howe

Maes Howe is the most famous of the Orkney Islands' prehistoric monuments. Visitors today who take the guided tour of the tomb (see www.historic-scotland.gov.uk for details) will find no treasure inside but they will enjoy one of the most memorable experiences offered by a megalithic monument anywhere in Britain. The confined 1.4-m (4.6-ft) high, 11-m (36-ft) long entrance passage suddenly opens out into a tall, corbel-vaulted central chamber, which soars some 3.8m (12.5ft) above your head. The corbelling (a method of roofing using flat, gradually overlapping stones) parallels exactly that used in the Newgrange tombs of the Boyne Valley in Ireland. Recent discoveries have indicated faint, scratched designs on the walls, which may have been guidelines for what could once have been a vividly painted interior. A large upright monolith stands at each corner of the chamber, while, to both sides, regular rectangular openings give access to small side cells. It is thought that these cells were used to inter the bones of the tomb's occupants. However, all that Farrer discovered was a single skull fragment.

It has been estimated that the construction of Maes Howe, which used 30 tonnes of Orcadian sandstone, would have taken 100,000 man-hours – an incredible feat of Neolithic organization as well as engineering.

Above: Aerial view of Maes Howe
Overleaf: Ring of Brodgar at dawn

The most recent theory about the origins of the tomb is that the encircling bank and ditch around the mound may have originated as a henge and stone circle. The massive stone slabs that form the side walls of the passage, and the monoliths at the corners of the chamber may all have been part of this original stone circle. This would match the remodelling that took place at other similar sites such as Stonehenge (see p.48–54) and Newgrange.

Ring of Brodgar

On an eastward-sloping plateau on the Ness o' Brodgar – the thin strip of land separating the Harray and Stenness lochs – stands the Ring of Brodgar stone circle, at the centre of a massive natural cauldron, formed by the hills in the surrounding landscape. Today, the spectacular site is accentuated by the glittering waters of the lochs, but when the ring was erected, perhaps between 2500 and 2000 BC, the Loch of Stenness didn't exist. In those days, the area was wet and marshy, surrounded by pools of water, or lochans. The sea breached the narrow landbridge at the Brig o' Waithe, filling the loch with saltwater, in around 1500 BC – at least 500 years after the ring was built.

Described as 'the finest known truly circular late Neolithic or early Bronze Age stone ring, and a later expression of the spirit which gave rise to Maes Howe, Stenness and Skara Brae' in the World Heritage Site nomination, Brodgar originally consisted of about 60 standing stones, of which only 27 remain today.

With a diameter of 104-m (341-ft), the Brodgar stone circle is the third largest in the British Isles. Covering an area of 8,435sq m (90,790sq ft), it is beaten only by the outer ring of stones at Avebury (see p.54–57) and the Greater Ring at Stanton Drew in England. In fact, the Brodgar circle is exactly the same size as Avebury's two inner circles. The perfect circle is enclosed within a massive, 105-m (344-ft) diameter, rock-cut ditch. With its two entrance causeways, one to the northwest, the other to the southeast, some archaeologists have classed the Ring of Brodgar, like Stonehenge and Avebury, as a henge monument.

The Brodgar stones vary in height from 2.1m (7ft) to a maximum of 4.7m (15.25ft). As the interior of the ring has never been fully excavated or scientifically dated, the actual time of its construction remains uncertain. However, the ring is generally assumed to have been the last of the great Neolithic monuments built on the Ness, and was part of an enormous prehistoric ritual complex that incorporated the Stones of Stenness to the southeast and, probably, the Ring of Bookan to the northwest. A short distance to the east of the Brodgar ring is the fluted, 1.75-m (5.75-ft) high solitary standing stone known as the Comet Stone.

Stones of Stenness

It is the sheer scale of the four elegant, blade-like standing stones, reaching a height of nearly 6m (20ft), that makes Stenness one of the most striking of Orkney's many prehistoric monuments.

Located on the southeastern shore of the Loch of Stenness, about a mile (1.6km) to the northwest of the Ring of Brodgar, the Stones of Stenness were originally laid out in around 3100 BC in the form of an ellipse, making it one of the earliest stone circles in Britain. The site was largely demolished in the early 19th century, since when the remaining stones have been re-erected. Excavations by the archaeologist Graham Ritchie in the 1970s suggested that the original circle of 12 stones was never, in fact, completed.

At the centre of the ring, there is a large stone hearth, similar to those found in Skara Brae and other Neolithic settlements. According to Dr Colin Richards, the excavator of the nearby Barnhouse Neolithic settlement, the hearth was constructed from four large stone slabs transported from Barnhouse. Close to the hearth, standing side by side, are two angular slabs with a large, prone stone beside them. This is the remains of the 'dolmen' that was mistakenly rebuilt – it had never formed part of the original complex – in 1906. As it was originally surrounded by a 44-m (144-ft) diameter, rock-cut ditch, the Stenness circle, like the neighbouring Ring of Brodgar, has been classed as a henge. It had a single entrance causeway on the north side, outside which there was a substantial earth bank, although little remains of either the bank or the ditch today.

Skara Brae

It's a humbling experience to step into one of the eight surviving dwellings of the Neolithic village of Skara Brae – one of Orkney's most-visited sites and one of the most remarkable prehistoric monuments in Europe. It gives you an unparalleled taste of what life was like on this windswept outpost of European civilization over 4,000 years ago. The buildings and their contents are incredibly well preserved thanks to the fact that they lay buried under sand until 1850, when a great winter storm exposed them. Not only are the walls of the houses still standing, and the low, covered alleyways between them still roofed with their original stone slabs, but the spartan interior stone furnishings of each house provide a unique time capsule of everyday life in Neolithic Orkney.

Each house has the same basic design – a large square room with a central hearth, a stone-built bed, which would have been lined with a heather or bracken 'mattress', on either side, and a shelved stone-slabbed 'dresser' on the wall opposite the doorway. The occupants would have lived off the cattle and sheep that they raised, plus the abundant seafood. But Skara Brae gradually became embedded in the rubbish created by its residents, and this, together with the ever-encroaching sand dunes, meant the village was slowly abandoned. It was finally buried under drifting sand, leaving it hidden from sight until the 19th century.

Skara Brae, which before its exposure was a large mound known as Skerrabra, stands on the southern shore of the beautiful Bay of Skaill, in the West Mainland parish of Sandwick. The first excavations were carried out in 1868 by the local laird, William Watt of Skaill, who uncovered the remains of four ancient houses. The settlement then remained undisturbed until 1925, when another storm damaged some of the structures. A sea wall was eventually built to preserve the village, and during this construction work more ancient buildings were discovered. Further excavations followed between 1928 and 1930, and, eventually, all the dwellings that we see today were uncovered. Radiocarbon-dating in the early 1970s confirmed that the settlement was late Neolithic, which means it was inhabited between 3200 BC and 2200 BC. The village remains under constant threat from coastal erosion and the twin onslaughts of sand and sea. In addition, the increasing number of visitors to the site each year are causing problems, although steps are being taken to minimize the damage.

Left: Box bed and fireplace inside a replica of a prehistoric dwelling at Skara Brae

St Kilda

... the future observer of St Kilda will be haunted the rest of his life by the place, and tantalized by the impossibility of describing it to those who have not seen it.
James Fisher, broadcaster and naturalist, 1947

After an often stormy crossing from Oban on the Scottish mainland, the approach to St Kilda, the most remote archipelago in the British Isles, is unforgettable. But then, the best places are often the most difficult to reach.

St Kilda is one of only 24 global locations to be awarded dual World Heritage Status, for both its natural and cultural significance. It was first inscribed for its 'outstanding natural features' in 1986 and, in 2004, the inscription was extended to include its surrounding pristine marine environment. St Kilda received further recognition the following year for its 2,000 years of human history and culture.

THE ST KILDA MAILBOAT

The first St Kilda mailboat was a distress signal sent out by a journalist, John Sands, who was on St Kilda when a nine-man Austrian ship foundered there in the winter of 1876. He wrote a letter asking for help and attached it to a life buoy from the stranded ship. It was picked up nine days later in Birsay, Orkney. Before that, the only way that St Kildans communicated with the outside world was to light a beacon on the 426m (1,389ft) summit of Conachair, in the hope that it might be seen by a passing ship. The islanders later developed Sands's idea, making small wooden boats from a cocoa tin, with the message secured inside, and using an inflated sheep's bladder as a float. The mailboat had the message 'Please Open' inscribed on it, and there was a small red flag tied to its mast. Subsequently, many mailboats were consigned to the sea and carried by the currents of the prevailing Gulf Stream, most eventually coming ashore on Orkney, the west coast of Scotland or Scandinavia. In later years, the mailboats were used by St Kildans as a tourist gimmick. Today, they are traditionally sent by National Trust for Scotland work parties as part of the ritual of visiting St Kilda. Records of mailboats and where they were washed up are regularly published in the St Kilda Mail, the journal of the NTS's St Kilda Club.

The crossing, via the Sound of Mull, west of Rum, through the Sound of Canna, northwest across the Minch, the sound of Harris and then due west, can take between 22 and 48 hours. One of the first visitors, Martin Martin in 1697, recorded: 'We proposed being at St Kilda next Day, but our Expectation was frustrated by a violent Storm, which almost drove us to the Ocean; where we incurred no small Risque, being no ways fitted for it; our Men laid aside all Hopes of Life…' John Reid, the experienced present-day skipper of the Jean de la Lune ferry, still talks about his boat doing the 'St Kilda Two-step' and the 'Ardnamurchan Waltz' in the tempestuous seas between St Kilda and the mainland.

St Kilda lies about 40 miles (66km) due west of Benbecula in Scotland's Outer Hebrides. As you leave the relative calm of the Sound of Harris, you may see tantalizing evidence of the archipelago – banners of white clouds often stream east in the prevailing wind from the still-invisible heights of Conachair on the main island of Hirta and Mullach an Eilein on Boreray to the west.

Eventually, about an hour after leaving the Isle of Shillay, you may just make out two faint black pyramids on the heaving horizon ahead. The larger, longer one to the left is Hirta; the one to the right is Boreray. Eventually, the misty shapes start to clarify and you'll start to pick out some of the individual islands: from left to right, the jagged ridge of Dun; Mullach Bi, Oiseval and Conachair on Hirta, with Soay beyond and, finally, Boreray, with the isolated peak of the precipitous sea stack of Stac an Armin on the extreme right.

The approach to Boreray, the first of the islands of the archipelago that you encounter, is a thrilling introduction to St Kilda. Passing under the beetling, 300-m (1,000-ft) high cliffs of Boreray is a mind-blowing experience, as thousands of screaming gannets from the world's largest breeding colony of these magnificent sea birds wheel around your head. On the steep, emerald green slopes of Mullach an Eilein, the grazing sheep are tiny white dots. Eventually, the whole of the archipelago is dramatically revealed between Boreray and the 191-m (626-ft) tall sea stack of Stac an Armin, one of the highest in Britain.

As the boat passes by the impossibly pointed fang of Stac Lee, rising some 165m (541ft) vertically from the sea and veined with guano-spattered terraces left by the colony of breeding gannets, you head for Hirta and the shelter of Village Bay, protected by the serrated natural breakwater of Dun.

The first sight of the deserted village, echoing the shape of the bay in a natural green ampitheatre under the slopes of Mullach Mor, is another memorable moment. The

Left: Stac an Armin and Boreray in the St Kilda archipelago
Overleaf: Aerial view of Hirta village, with the natural breakwater of Dun sheltering
Village Bay

layout of the 19th-century village remains to this day, with the grey, mostly roofless ruins imparting a real sense of melancholy. Over 1,400 cleitean (dry-stone-built storehouses) for keeping food and fuel are scattered like sheep all over the slopes of Mullach Mor and on the other islands, some even on the isolated sea stacks.

The spirit of the former St Kildans, eventually driven from their homes by the unsustainable nature of their life here in 1930, seems to pervade every building. You are probably most aware of this in the restored kirk, which was originally built in 1830, and the schoolroom, where there is a small exhibition alongside the evocative desks of the teacher and pupils.

Natural history

St Kilda's exceptional cliffs and sea stacks form the most important sea bird breeding site in northwest Europe and one of the best in the North Atlantic. The world's largest colony of gannets, over 60,000 strong, nests on the precipitous ledges of Boreray and its adjacent sea stacks. St Kilda also has the largest colony of fulmars in the British Isles – nearly 65,000 were counted in 1999 – and there are around 230,000 apparently occupied burrows of the comical, clown-like puffins on the islands.

The brown-fleeced, goat-like Soay sheep, which take their name from the island of Soay, meaning 'sheep island', are a unique primitive breed that dates back to the Bronze Age. Soay sheep are not sheared in the normal way, but 'rooed', or plucked, with a knife. DNA samples extracted from Soay sheep on St Kilda have enabled

Above left: Soay sheep
Above right: A pair of fulmars at the nest

researchers to compare the genetic make-up of the sheep and their survival rate. Because of their frugal dietary requirements, Soay sheep are much in demand for conservation projects throughout Britain.

St Kilda is still the home of two distinct subspecies of creatures – the St Kilda field mouse and the St Kilda wren. There was also a St Kilda house mouse but it became extinct after the islanders left in 1930. The mice were larger subspecies of the mainland house mouse and wood mouse, and were probably brought to St Kilda in the longboats of visiting Vikings. The St Kilda wren, a larger subspecies of the mainland wren, is found throughout the archipelago. There are believed to be about 120 pairs on Hirta, usually nesting in the stone-built cleitean.

Human history

Evidence of the first human settlement of St Kilda is provided by the boat-shaped stone settings of An Lag above the deserted village on Hirta. These date back to around 1850 BC. The purpose of these large stones set on their edges is still unknown – they may have been graves but no human remains have ever been found in them.

Also on Hirta is the Earth House, or House of the Fairies (*Taigh an t-Sithiche*), a souterrain, or underground passage, which dates back to between 500 BC and AD 300. Excavations in 1876 unearthed large quantities of burnt limpet shells and the bones of sheep, cattle and sea birds, such as fulmars and gannets. It may have been an ice house for the storage of food.

In the north of the island, in green Gleann Mor, or the Great Glen, lie the remains of what is known as the Amazon's House. This consists of a large 'horned' forecourt leading to a single enclosure with three cells. It is named after the legend of an Amazon who crossed the land bridge that existed then between the islands of the archipelago and the Outer Hebrides to go hunting, driving the deer back towards Harris and Lewis for killing.

The population of St Kilda, which at its height stood at 200, traditionally caught gannets, fulmars and puffins for food, feathers and oil. During the breeding season, from about March to September, the birds were taken either by hand or with a fowling rod or a snare by nimble-footed islanders who descended the vertical faces of the stacks on a rope, sometimes even crawling along the tiny ledges where the birds nested at night. Some of the birds were consumed, with the remainder going as rent to the landowners, the MacLeod clan and, later, the Marquess of Bute. At one time, it was estimated that each person on St Kilda ate 115 fulmars every year; in 1876, it was said that the islanders caught 89,600 puffins for food and feathers.

Left: Boreray, an uninhabited island in the St Kilda archipelago

The skills of the St Kildan sea cliff climbers were legendary. Martin observed in 1697: '... necessity has made them apply themselves to this, and custom has perfected them in it; so that it is become familiar to them almost from their cradles, the young boys of three years old begin to climb the walls of their houses.' The boys grew up with no fear of heights, and were on the crags by the age of ten or 11. By the time they were 16, they were fully fledged cragsmen on the highest sea cliffs in Britain.

Gradually, though, the St Kildans became less self-sufficient, relying on imports of food, fuel and building materials and furnishings for their homes. In 1852, 36 people emigrated to Australia, reducing the population to 74, with only 14 men over 20 years old. Many of the emigrants died *en route*, but a few did reach Melbourne, where they settled. A suburb of the city is still called St Kilda.

The steady decline in the population continued, and islanders felt increasingly isolated from the outside world, suffering particularly from a lack of regular communication with it. In 1912, there were acute food shortages, and an outbreak of influenza devastated the islands a year later. World War I brought a naval detachment to Hirta, and with it regular deliveries of mail and food from naval supply vessels. When these services were withdrawn at the end of the war, the feelings of isolation increased. More able-bodied young islanders emigrated and, eventually, there was a breakdown of the island economy. In 1930, the remaining 36 islanders asked the Government to be evacuated to the mainland, so bringing to a poignant end an extraordinary story of survival.

The sad story of the islanders after their evacuation on HMS *Harebell* on 28 August 1930 is movingly told in Charles Maclean's *Island on the Edge of the World* (1972). 'Most went as planned to live in Morvern, Argyllshire and work for the Forestry Commission, but they lacked the determination to begin life afresh... Trees were not something the islanders knew much about, but that could not be helped, they would learn.' Many of the older islanders died soon after arriving on the mainland, and others stayed homesick for the rest of their lives, returning to St Kilda in the summer to live in their old homes.

In 1931, St Kilda was sold to the Marquess of Bute, a keen ornithologist. He bequeathed it to the National Trust for Scotland in 1957. Today, three organizations – the NTS, Scottish Natural Heritage and the Ministry of Defence – work in partnership in a programme of conservation and research to ensure the continuing care and protection of this unique World Heritage Site.

Giant's Causeway Coast, County Antrim

Boswell: 'Is not the Giant's Causeway worth seeing?'
Johnson: 'Worth seeing? Yes, but not worth going to see.'

Samuel Johnson, the 18th-century poet, critic and writer, was fairly dismissive of the Giant's Causeway, if his biographer, James Boswell, in his *Life of Samuel Johnson* of 1791, is to be believed. And novelist William Makepeace Thackeray was equally unimpressed 50 years later, when he arrived to see it in a very small boat on a wild and stormy day, as he described in his *Irish Sketch Book* of 1842:

'That's the Causeway before you,' says the guide.
'Which?'
'That pier which you see jutting out into the bay, right ahead.'
'Mon Dieu! and I have travelled a hundred and fifty miles to see that?'

THE MIGHTY FINN

Long ago, a fierce giant named Finn MacCool roamed the north coast of Ireland now known as Antrim. From here, he could look across the Sea of Moyle to Scotland, where his great rival, the Scottish giant Benandonner, was a constant threat. The two giants had never met, so Finn invited Benandonner to Ireland to challenge him to a decisive battle. So that he had no excuse to avoid the confrontation, Finn built a causeway of huge stones across the water so that the Scottish giant could travel on dry land. As Benandonner approached the Irish coast, Finn realized that his opponent was much larger and more fearsome than he had anticipated, and he fled to his home in the nearby hills. Fortunately for Finn, his wife Oonagh was an ingenious woman. She disguised him as a baby in a large nightgown and bonnet, and then placed him in a huge, hastily made cradle, telling him to pretend to be asleep as Benandonner knocked at the door. Oonagh invited the Scottish giant in for tea, pleading with him not to waken Finn's child. Glancing at the massive 'baby' lying in the cradle, Benandonner took fright, saying that if this were the child, he had no wish to meet the father. He fled back to Scotland, ripping up the causeway behind him so that the mighty Finn could not follow...

In fairness, many people's first impression of County Antrim's world-famous geological showplace is that it is much smaller than expected. However, the Giant's Causeway is merely the centrepiece of a fascinating 175-acre site that extends for 4 miles (6km) along the bay-indented Antrim coast. At Benbane Head, the northernmost point of Northern Ireland, the soaring cliffs rise to 300ft (90m). The Causeway is said to constitute the largest ancient lava plateau in Europe, and is rich in folklore and legend (see box, left).

Lying about 7 miles (12km) east of Portrush, the Giant's Causeway became Ireland's first World Heritage site in November 1986. It met two of UNESCO's criteria: as a prime example of earth's evolutionary history during the Tertiary period, and the fact that it contained rare and superlative natural phenomena.

How the Causeway was formed

The basalt rocks of the Giant's Causeway were formed during the Tertiary period, about 50–60 million years ago, as a result of volcanic activity. The viscous lava from nearby eruptions flowed into a depression, forming a sort of inland lava lake. As it cooled, the lava hardened, shrunk and finally cracked to form the approximately

Left: Giant's Causeway
Above: The Giant's Boot, an oddity near the Causeway
Overleaf: Sunset on the basalt columns of the Giant's Causeway

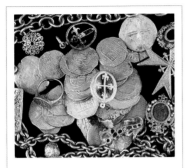

40,000 mainly hexagonal columns of black basalt rock running out into the sea that we see today.

The bottom layer of these rocks is, logically, known as the Lower Basalt. After two million years of a warm, wet climate, this lower basalt has weathered to create a deep red rock called laterite, which is most noticeable near the curving formation known as the Giant's Harp. As more volcanic eruptions occurred, more lava poured onto the red rock, cooling and hardening to form the Causeway, or the Middle Basalt. The Upper Basalt formed during the last period of volcanic activity, but most of this layer was eroded away during the last Ice Age, about 15,000 years ago.

There are a number of spectacular features along the Causeway Coast, many related to the legend of Finn MacCool (see box, p.201). These include the Giant's Boot, a detached boot-shaped formation on the shore; the Giant's Organ at Port Noffer; the Giant's Harp, above Port Reostan; and the adjacent so-called Chimney Pots, where some of the tottering basaltic columns have become detached from the cliffs.

Europe's first hydro-electric tram, designed by William Traill and opened in 1883, ran between Portrush and the Causeway Hotel. It was affectionately known as 'the toast rack' because of its quaintly shaped carriages. For many people, the rattling, leisurely tram journey around the spectacular coast was the highlight of their holiday. The last section of the tramway finally closed in 1951.

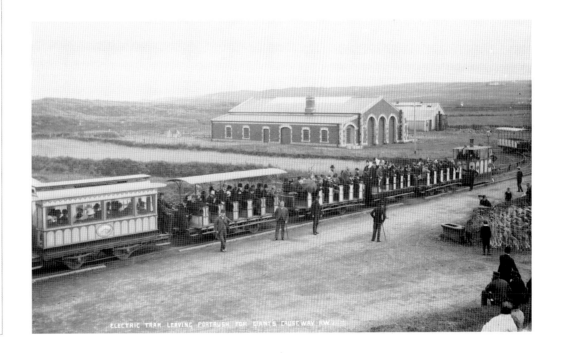

Left: The Giant's Organ at Port Noffer
Above: The hydro-electric tram, known as the Toast Rack

Conclusion:
A badge of honour

Heritage is our legacy from the past, what we live with today, and what we pass on to future generations. Our cultural and natural heritage are both irreplaceable sources of life and inspiration.

From *The World's Heritage* by UNESCO (2009)

When the Pontcysyllte Aqueduct and Llangollen Canal (see p.118) in North Wales was inscribed as Britain's latest World Heritage Site in 2009 at the 33rd session of UNESCO's World Heritage Committee, it was the culmination of more than six years of local campaigning.

Dr Dawn Roberts, economic development manager for Wrexham County Borough Council, spoke for many when she said: 'We are absolutely over the moon. We have been working on this for so long and it means so much to those of us who are from this area. To have our aqueduct and our canal named as a World Heritage Site is amazing.' And she added: 'World Heritage status does not bring with it any prize or money, it is more of a badge of honour. It is an awesome sight and one of those sites in the world we feel people must visit.' That's the essence of World Heritage Site status. There is no monetary reward, financial advantage, nor political kudos. It is just having your site recognized by a respected international body of experts that it is of special, global importance. And, as the people of Wrexham found, that 'badge of honour' means an awful lot.

Pontcysyllte was Britain's only nomination in 2009, but there are plenty of other sites that would love to join the 25 currently on UNESCO's British list. Some may not have quite the same 'outstanding universal value' of the Great Wall of China, the Taj Mahal or the Grand Canyon, but many prospective sites are nevertheless outstanding examples of natural history and culture, which could hold their own against any elsewhere in the world.

The Tentative List

As explained in the Introduction, the first step a country must take to obtain World Heritage Site status is to make an inventory of what it considers to be its important natural and cultural heritage sites. This inventory, known as the Tentative List, provides a forecast of the properties that a country may decide to submit for inscription in the next five to ten years, and it may be updated at any time.

Right: Pontcysyllte Aqueduct

At the time of writing, there are 15 British sites on this list, including no fewer than three national parks: the Lake District, the New Forest and the Cairngorms. There are also two sites outside the geographical scope of this book: Fountain Cavern in Anguilla, in the Leeward Islands of the Caribbean, and the defences of the Rock of Gibraltar at the mouth of the Mediterranean. The Lake District in Cumbria and the twin Saxon monastic sites of Wearmouth and Jarrow in Tyne and Wear have well-developed bids and both are hoping for inscription by 2012.

The Lake District World Heritage Site Steering Group, a partnership of local and national organizations, was set up in 2005 to pursue its mixed cultural and natural site bid. The group's purpose in taking forward the nomination to the UK Government and UNESCO, currently planned for 2011, is to produce wider social and economic benefits for the area.

The Lake District is England's largest and best-loved national park, covering 885sq miles (2,292sq km) of mountains and lakes in the northwest corner of the country. It has long been valued for its natural beauty and appreciated as an example of man's harmonious interaction with the natural environment. It has also had a profound influence on the artistic appreciation of the beauties of nature, inspiring Wordsworth and the other Lake Poets, as well as many of Britain's finest landscape painters.

The twin Saxon monasteries of Wearmouth and Jarrow were founded in the 7th century by Benedict Biscop. The Venerable Bede, the original British historian who was a member of the monastic community from the age of seven, described them

as 'one monastery in two places'. In its day, it was one of the world's greatest cultural centres.

The monastery had one of the best libraries in Europe, giving Bede, Wearmouth-Jarrow's most famous scholar, access to ideas from all over the world. Two centuries before there was a united England, Bede was the first person to write a history of the English people, and, among many other things, he popularized the use of 'BC' and 'AD' in the recording of dates.

The boundary of the nominated site includes the Anglo-Saxon monastery, the medieval priory and St Peter's church at Wearmouth, and at Jarrow, St Paul's church and churchyard, Drewett's Park, Jarrow Hall and parts of the banks of the River Don.

Other British sites on UNESCO's Tentative List include Chatham Naval Dockyard on the north Kent coast. This is perhaps the best example of a royal dockyard, largely unaltered from the age of sail, when the Royal Navy was vital to Britain's global influence and when dockyards were the largest industrial centres in Europe. The dockyard, defended by what are known as the Brompton Lines, contained everything necessary to build, repair, maintain and equip ships, and was supplemented by the Board of Ordnance's facilities for the supply of guns, ammunition and powder to the navy and army.

Near by are the barracks for the army and marines, which were served by the village of Brompton. The most significant of these are the Board of Ordnance's Brompton Artillery Barracks (1806), which now form the School of Military Engineering of the Royal Engineers. The proposed World Heritage Site focuses on the 18th- and early 19th-century dockyard.

Also in Kent is the home of Charles Darwin, the man who came up with what has been described as 'the greatest idea' of the theory of evolution by natural selection. Darwin's Home and Workplace: Down House and Environs was his home from 1842 until his death in 1882. Here, he wrote his masterpiece *On the Origin of Species: By Means of Natural Selection*, first published in 1859 and never out of print since.

The grounds and surrounding landscape, including the strip of woodland containing the Sand Walk, Darwin's famous 'thinking path', provided the inspiration for his revolutionary insights into the natural world, ecology and bio-diversity, which continue to have profound influence today. Despite its close proximity to London, Down House, a Grade I listed building, has retained the rural charm that first attracted Darwin. A conservation and display project completed by English Heritage in 1998 preserved the fabric of Darwin's home, re-creating the interior and the atmosphere in which he worked.

Manchester in the northwest of England is the archetypal city of the Industrial Revolution. It witnessed the creation of Britain's first industrial canal, its first mainline, intercity passenger railway, and was home to the country's first industrial suburb based on steam power. The proposed World Heritage Site of Manchester and Salford (including Ancoats, Castlefield and Worsley) focuses on these three themes, and the site is linked by the Bridgewater and Rochdale Canals. The Bridgewater Canal, designed by James Brindley and opened to Manchester in 1765, was the first true industrial canal.

From the Castlefield Conservation Area, the proposed site follows the Rochdale Canal, the first canal to cross the Pennines (opening in 1804) to Ancoats, which had developed from 1794 in expectation of the arrival of the canal. The industrialization of Ancoats under the impetus provided by steam power was dramatic even by Manchester's standards, so that by 1849 it was stated that 'Ancoats... is to Manchester what Manchester is to England'.

The third element in the development of the site came with the arrival of George Stephenson's Liverpool and Manchester Railway in 1830. Its terminus, the oldest mainline station in the world, survives in Liverpool Road, backed by some of the earliest purpose-built railway warehouses in the world. The Liverpool and Manchester Railway was a spectacular commercial success, serving as a model for railway entrepreneurs throughout Europe and in North America.

Another potential British World Heritage Site, which is based on the nation's transport revolution in the 19th century, is selected parts of the Great Western Railway, between Paddington and Bristol. The railway was authorized by Parliament in 1835, and opened in 1841. It was the creation of engineering genius Isambard Kingdom Brunel and was to be, in his own words, 'the finest work in the kingdom'.

It includes the 2-mile (2.9-km) Box Tunnel with its massive entrance portals, perhaps the greatest feat of early railway engineering construction; the termini at Paddington and Bristol Temple Meads; the entrance to the World Heritage city of Bath (see p.22) via the turreted Twerton Tunnels and a long viaduct; the Swindon Railway Works and village, now incoporating the National Monuments Record Centre; the magnificent bridge over the Thames at Maidenhead; and the Wharncliffe Viaduct at Hanwell. The survival of these, and many other lesser structures, combine to make the Great Western Railway the most complete railway line from its time in the world.

Mount Stewart Gardens, on the shores of Strangford Lough in Northern Ireland, is one of the most spectacular and individual gardens of Western Europe. It's renowned for the 'extraordinary scope of its plant collections and the originality of its features, which give it world-class status'. It was created in 1921 by Edith, Lady Londonderry, with advice from such eminent gardeners as Gertrude Jekyll and Sir John Ross.

Features of the formal gardens in the 80-acre nominated area include the Sunk Garden, designed by Gertrude Jekyll; the Italian garden; the Dodo Terrace, with its humorous statuary representing family friends and political figures; the Spanish Garden, noted for its fine loggia and arches of Monterey cypress; and the Shamrock Garden, which incorporates some fine topiary.

The names of Stratford-upon-Avon and William Shakespeare are synonymous throughout the world, and they are both celebrated in the proposed Shakespeare's Stratford World Heritage Site. Shakespeare, the world's greatest dramatist, was born and brought up, educated, met and married his wife and baptized his children in Stratford. Many properties linked to his life are run by the Shakespeare Birthplace Trust here and are open to the public. The town was also where he invested most of his theatrical earnings, where he retired and died, and where he was buried, in Holy Trinity parish church.

The site encompasses most of the historic core of Stratford, and includes key buildings directly associated with Shakespeare and his family, including his birthplace in Henley Street. It also includes two later buildings where his legacy is kept alive: the Royal Shakespeare Theatre, and the adjoining Swan Theatre and Shakespeare

Above: The Rochdale Canal at Castleford
Overleaf: Loch Avon in the Cairngorms National Park

Centre. There are two other atmospheric places just outside the town with strong Shakespearian connections: Anne Hathaway's (his wife's) Cottage at Shottery, and Mary Arden's (his mother's) House at Wilmcote.

Among the natural sites included on the British Tentative List are the semi-Arctic Cairngorm Mountains in northeastern Scotland. These are the largest continuous area of high ground above 1,000m (3,200ft) in Britain and contain most of the highest summits in Scotland. The Cairngorms were made a national park in 2003.

The mountains, with their distinctive plateaux and glacially sculptured features, are surrounded by open moorland and deep glens. Such a diverse assembly of features in a relatively compact area is exceptional on both a western European and international level. In this respect, the Cairngorms have been compared with parts of Baffin Island in Arctic Canada.

The peatlands of the Flow Country of Caithness and Sutherland in the far north of Scotland are probably the largest single area of blanket bog in the world. Together with associated areas of moorland and open water, they are of international importance for conservation, both as a habitat in their own right and because they support a wide range of rare and unusual breeding birds.

Also in Scotland is the Forth Rail Bridge, which was opened in 1890 and is probably the best-known rail bridge in the world. Designed by John Fowler and Benjamin Baker and built by the Glasgow-based company Sir William Arrol & Co to provide a rail link across the River Firth between the Lothians and Fife, it was the first major steel bridge in Europe. The Forth Bridge is now an internationally recognized symbol of the achievements of late 19th-century engineering.

Since 1964, a road bridge has shared the same crossing point as the Forth Bridge, which is just longer than the Severn Bridge in Avon, and remained the longest suspension bridge in the UK until the Humber Bridge near Kingston-upon-Hull opened in 1981. The proposed World Heritage Site encompasses the bridge and the designated conservation areas in North and South Queensferry on either side.

The New Forest on the south coast in Hampshire is an area of outstanding wildlife and landscape interest, shaped by human use over thousands of years. The proposed site extends to about 224sq miles (580sq km) and is based on the New Forest Heritage Area. The New Forest, which was originally set aside by William the Conqueror as a royal hunting preserve as long ago as 1079, was designated as Britain's latest national park in 2005.

The quality of the New Forest's habitats and landscapes, particularly of the unenclosed areas, is dependent on a pastoral economy, based on the exercise of common grazing rights. This economy relies on the continued existence of a small community of about 400 commoners, governed by a court of verderers. The landscape of the New Forest includes old woodlands, timber plantations of different types, extensive tracts of heathland (which make up the largest single unit of continuous lowland heath in Europe), lowland bogs, grassy lawns, enclosed farmland, large estates, coastland, and a number of villages and small towns.

The Wash and North Norfolk Coast is an area of international nature conservation importance. Covering an area of 270sq miles (700sq km), it is designated a Ramsar site, a wetland of international importance under the Ramsar Convention, especially as a habitat for visiting wildfowl.

The proposed site is made up of intertidal sands and muds, shingle, sand dunes, lagoons and salt marshes. The Wash estuary is a complex ecosystem, while the North Norfolk coast is one of the finest coastlines in Britain and one of the few European examples of a barrier coast. It is also recognized for its landscape importance, designated as an Area of Outstanding Natural Beauty (AONB) and as a Heritage Coast, and encompassing several National Nature Reserves (NNRs) and Sites of Special Scientific Interest (SSSIs).

Where next?

The choice of the inscription of World Heritage Sites is obviously subjective and sometimes frankly arbitrary. Some sites are obvious and unquestionable, while others seem to have been decided for political reasons, as a result of effective local campaigning, or maybe to fend off a perceived threat, such as in the case of Abu Simbel, where we began our journey.

Some people have asked why, if the cities of Bath, Durham and Edinburgh have been inscribed, have not Oxford, Cambridge or York, cities with equal historic and cultural connections? Durham Cathedral was included in the Durham designation, and Westminster Abbey in that of the Palace of Westminster, while Canterbury Cathedral was inscribed on its own merits. So why not Salisbury, Winchester and St Paul's Cathedrals, surely equally fine examples of globally important ecclesiastical architecture?

And if Blenheim, Versailles and Fontainebleau, why not Hampton Court Palace, Windsor Castle and Chatsworth? Indeed, if Mont-St-Michel and its bay was considered suitable, why not its cousin across the Channel, St Michael's Mount in Cornwall?

There's no glib and simple answer to these questions. Koïchiro Matsuura, former director general of UNESCO, perhaps explained the situation about World Heritage Site inscription best in his foreword to *The World's Heritage* in 2009.

'Although every year new sites are inscribed by the World Heritage Committee, many sites of outstanding value have yet to be included on the List, which strives to ensure a true representation of the full diversity of all types of tangible heritage. The open-ended nature of the List is precisely what makes it such a vibrant instrument for preservation.'

Tentative UK World Heritage Sites

- Chatham Naval Dockyard, Kent
- Darwin's Home and Workplace: Down House and Environs
- Lake District, Cumbria
- Manchester and Salford (Ancoats, Castlefield and Worsley)
- Wearmouth and Jarrow Monastic Sites, Tyne and Wear
- Mount Stewart Gardens, Northern Ireland
- Shakespeare's Stratford
- The Cairngorm Mountains
- The Flow Country
- The Forth Rail Bridge
- The Great Western Railway: Paddington–Bristol (selected parts)
- The New Forest, Hampshire
- The Wash and North Norfolk Coast

Useful Addresses

The West

The World Heritage Centre
United Nations Educational, Scientific and
Cultural Organization
7 place de Fontenoy
75352 Paris 07 SP, France
Tel: +33-(0)1-45 68 15 71
Email: wh-info@unesco.org
Website: whc.unesco.org

City of Bath
Bath Tourist Information Centre
Abbey Chambers, Abbey Churchyard
Bath BA1 1LY
Tel: 0906 711 2000
Email: tourism@bathtourism.co.uk
Website: www.visitbath.co.uk

Cornwall & West Devon Mines
Cornish Mining World Heritage Site Office
The Percuil Building
Cornwall Council, Old County Hall
Truro, Cornwall TR1 3AY
Tel: 01872 322586
Email: kwillows@cornwall.gov.uk
Website: www.cornish-mining.org.uk

Dorset & East Devon Coast
Jurassic Coast Team
Dorset County Council
County Hall, Colliton Park
Dorchester, Dorset DT1 1XJ
Tel: 01305 251000
Email: sam.rose@dorsetcc.gov.uk
Website: www.jurassiccoast.com

Stonehenge, Avebury & Associated sites
English Heritage
South West Regional Office
29 Queen Square, Bristol BS1 4ND
Tel: 0117 975 0700
Email: southwest@english-heritage.org.uk
Website: www.english-heritage.org.uk

Canterbury Cathedral
Cathedral House, 11 The Precincts,
Canterbury, Kent, CT1 2EH
Tel: 01227 762862
Email: enquiries@canterbury-cathedral.org
Website: www.canterbury-cathedral.org

The South

Maritime Greenwich
Greenwich Tourist Information Centre
46 Greenwich Church Street
Greenwich, London, SE10 9BL
Tel: 0870 608 2000
Email: tic@greenwich.gov.uk
Website: www.greenwichwhs.org.uk

Royal Botanic Gardens, Kew
Richmond, Surrey, TW9 3AB
Tel: 020 8332 5655
Email: info@kew.org
Website: www.kew.org

Tower of London
London EC3N 4AB
Tel: 0844 482 7777
Email: visitorservices_TOL@hrp.org.uk
Website: www.hrp.org.uk/toweroflondon

Westminster Palace & Abbey
The Chapter Office
Westminster Abbey, 20 Dean's Yard
London SW1P 3PA
Tel: 020 7222 5152
Email: info@westminster-abbey.org
Website: www.westminster-abbey.org

The Palace of Westminster
House of Commons
London SW1A 0AA
Tel: 020 7219 4272
Email: hcinfo@parliament.uk
Website: www.parliament.uk

The Midlands

Blenheim Palace
Woodstock
Oxfordshire OX20 1PP
Tel: 01993 811091
Freephone: 0800 849 6500 (24-hour info service)
Email: operations@blenheimpalace.com
Website: www.blenheimpalace.com

Derwent Valley Mills
Derwent Valley Mills World Heritage Site Office
PO Box 6297, Matlock
Derbyshire DE4 3WJ
Tel: 01629 533363
Email: adrian.farmer@derbyshire.gov.uk
Website: www.derwentvalleymills.org

Ironbridge Gorge
Ironbridge Gorge Museum Trust
Coach Road, Coalbrookdale
Telford TF8 7DQ
Tel: 01952 884391

Email: library@ironbridge.org.uk
Website: www.ironbridge.org.uk

Wales

Blaenavon Co-ordinating Officer
c/o Development Department
Torfaen County Borough Council
County Hall
Cwmbran NP44 2WN
Tel: 01633 648317
Website: www.world-heritage-blaenavon.org.uk

Pontcysyllte Aqueduct
c/o British Waterways, Navigation Road, Llangollen,
Cheshire CW8 1BH
Tel: 01606 723800
Email: enquiries.wbc@britishwaterways.co.uk
Website: www.waterscape.com; www.drifters.co.uk

Welsh Edwardian Castles
Cadw
Welsh Assembly Government
Plas Carew, Unit 5/7 Cefn Coed
Parc Nantgarw, Cardiff CF15 7QQ
Tel: 01443 33 6000
Email: cadw@wales.gsi.gov.uk
Website: www.cadw.wales.gov.uk

The North

Durham Cathedral & Castle
Tourist Information Centre
2 Millennium Place
Durham DH1 1WA
Tel: 0191 384 3720
Email: touristinfo@durhamcity.gov.uk
Website: www.durhamtourism.co.uk

Hadrian's & Antonine Wall
Hadrian's Wall Heritage Ltd
East Peterel Field
Dipton Mill Road
Hexham
Northumberland, NE46 2JT
Tel: 01434 609700
Email: nigel.mills@hadrianswallheritage.co.uk
Website: www.hadrians-wall.org

Liverpool
Liverpool City Centre Tourist Information Centre
The 08 Place, Whitechapel
Liverpool L1 6DZ
Tel: 0151 2332008
Email: 08place@liverpool.gov.uk
Website: www.visitliverpool.com

Saltaire
Salts Mill, Shipley, Saltaire
West Yorkshire BD18 3LA
Tel: 01274 531163
Email: admin@saltairevillage.info
Website: www.saltairevillage

Studley Royal Park & Fountains Abbey
Fountains Abbey & Studley Royal Water Garden
Ripon, Nr Harrogate
North Yorkshire HG4 3DY
Tel: 01765 608888
Email: fountainsenquiries@nationaltrust.org.uk
Website: www.fountainsabbey.org.uk

Scotland & Northern Ireland

Edinburgh
VisitScotland
Ocean Point One, 94 Ocean Drive
Edinburgh EH6 6JH
Tel: 0845 225 5121
Email: info@visitscotland.com
Website: www.edinburgh.org

New Lanark
New Lanark World Heritage Site Office
South Lanarkshire ML11 9DB
Tel: 01555 661345
Email: trust@newlanark.org
Website: www.newlanark.org

Neolithic Orkney
VisitOrkney
The Travel Centre
West Castle Street
Kirkwall
Orkney KW15 1GU
Tel: 01856 872856
Email: info@visitorkney.com
Website: www.visitorkney.com or www.orkneyjar.com

St Kilda
The National Trust for Scotland
28 Charlotte Square, Edinburgh EH2 4ET
Tel: 0844 493 2100
Email: information@nts.org
Website: www.kilda.org.uk

Giant's Causeway Coast
Giant's Causeway Visitor Centre
44 Causeway Road, Bushmills
Co Antrim BT57 8SU
Tel: 028 2073 1855
Email: info@giantscausewaycentre.com
Website: www.giantscausewaycentre.com

Index

Acknowledgements

The author would like to thank Griff Rhys Jones for writing the foreword; Steve Knightley for permission to use the lyrics of *Cousin Jack* on page 30; Paul Mitchell for commissioning the book; Patrick Budge, Phil Barfoot and Alice Earle for making it look so attractive; and 'pesky' copy editor Helen Ridge and editor Donna Wood for their good-humoured editing of it. As ever, the author thanks his wife, Val, for her unstinting support and forbearance during the research and writing.

The Automobile Association would like to thank the following photographers, companies and picture libraries for their assistance in the preparation of this book.

Abbreviations for the picture credits are as follows: (t) top; (b) bottom; (l) left; (r) right; (c) centre; b/g background; (AA) AA World Travel Library;

Trade cover: Front & spine: Alan Copson/JAI/Corbis, Back: AA/Michael Moody; SS cover: Front & spine: David Paterson/Photographer's Choice/Getty Images, Back: Stephen Emerson/Alamy; Back flap: AA/Steve Day; Endpaper: Sandro Vannini/Corbis; 1 AA/Caroline Jones; 5 b/g Frank Siteman/Science Faction/Corbis; 6 AA/Michael Moody; 7 Geoffrey Swaine/Rex Features; 9t Keystone/Getty Images; 9b AA/Rick Strange; 10-11 Ine Beerten/Alamy; 14 AA/A Mockford & N Bonetti; 17 AA/A Mockford & N Bonetti; 19 UNESCO/World Heritage Centre; 20 Rosine Mazin/Photolibrary; 22t Mary Evans Picture Library; 22c AA/Steve Day; 23 AA/Caroline Jones; 24-25 AA/Caroline Jones; 26 James Osmond/Photolibrary; 27 akg-images/PictureContact; 28bl Mary Evans Picture Library; 28t Victoria Art Gallery, Bath and North East Somerset Council/The Bridgeman Art Library; 29 AA/Caroline Jones; 30 Mary Evans Picture Library/Alamy; 32-33 AA/Adam Burton; 34 Geevor Tin Mine Archive; 36bl Georgia Glynn Smith/Photolibrary; 36t Daniel Crowe/Alamy; 37 View Pictures Ltd/Alamy; 39bl Private Collection/The Bridgeman Art Library; 39tr Tomas Bravo/Reuters/Corbis; 40-41 Guy Edwardes/Photolibrary; 43 British Geological Survey (P666957) photograph by permission of BGS © NERC 2010; 44 Stephen Emerson/Alamy; 47 Jinny Goodman/Alamy; 48 Jason Hawkes/Corbis; 50-51 AA/Michael Moody; 52 Salisbury & South Wiltshire Museum/The Bridgeman Art Library; 53 Private Collection/Look and Learn/The Bridgeman Art Library; 54 Jane Brayne/Wessex Archaeology; 55 Flight Images LLP/Photolibrary; 56 AA/Michael Moody; 57 AA/Michael Moody; 58 Richard Osbourne/Alamy; 59 Andrew Parker/Alamy; 60l Private Collection/Ken Welsh/The Bridgeman Art Library; 60b Peter de Clercq/Alamy; 61 The Print Collector/Alamy; 62 Ethel Davies/Photolibrary; 63bl Private Collection/The Bridgeman Art Library; 63tr Wendy White/Alamy; 64 The Print Collector/Alamy; 65 National Maritime Museum, Greenwich, London; 66-67 AA/Neil Setchfield; 68 National Maritime Museum, Greenwich, London; 69 National Maritime Museum, Greenwich, London; 70bl AA/Neil Setchfield; 70t Maurice Savage/Alamy; 71 Mike Booth/Alamy; 72 Bruce McGowan/Alamy; 73 World History Archive/Alamy; 74-75 Gregory Wrona/Alamy; 76 Steve Taylor ARPS/Alamy; 77bl David Ball/Alamy; 77tr Robert Harding Picture Library Ltd/Alamy; 78bl AA/Sarah Montgomery; 78tr National Gallery, London, UK/The Bridgeman Art Library; 79tl Private Collection/Look and Learn/The Bridgeman Art Library; 79br AA/Wyn Voysey; 80bl TNT Magazine/Alamy; 81 AA/Wyn Voysey; 82 AA/James Tims; 83 Illustrated London News Ltd/Mary Evans; 84-85 AA; 86 AA/James Tims; 87 AA/Neil Setchfield; 88 Skyscan/Corbis; 89 Beata Moore/Alamy; 90 Jason Hawkes/Corbis; 91bl SuperStock/Getty; 91tr Reproduced with the kind permission of His Grace the Duke of Marlborough; 93 Jon Bower UK/Alamy; 94 Robin Weaver/Alamy; 95 The Art Gallery Collection/Alamy; 96 Dave Porter/Photolibrary; 97t Derby Museum and Art Gallery, UK/The Bridgeman Art Library; 97c Science & Society Picture Library/Getty; 98 Private Collection/Philip Mould Ltd, London/The Bridgeman Art Library; 99 Robert Morris/Alamy; 100 Skyscan Photolibrary/Alamy; 101 Daniel Bosworth/Photolibrary; 102-103 Pawel Libera/Photolibrary; 104 Science Museum Pictorial; 105t Craig Holmes Premium/Alamy; 105c Sandro Vannini/Corbis; 105b David Bagnall/Alamy; 106 Steve Frost/Alamy; 107 David Levenson/Alamy; 108 Keith Morris/Alamy; 109 Graham Morley/PhotolibraryWales; 111b Judith Davies; 111tr Matt Botwood (CStock)/Alamy; 112-113 Nigel Forster/PhotolibraryWales; 114 Jeff Morgan 04/Alamy; 115t Science Museum Pictorial; 115b Chris Howes/Wild Places Photography/Alamy; 117 Amgueddfa Cymru National Museum Wales; 118tl Mary Evans Picture Library/Ins. of Civil Engineers; 118b Steve Lewis/Photolibrary; 120 AA/Mark Bauer; 122 By permission of Llyfrgell Genedlaethol Cymru/National Library of Wales; 123 Mary Evans Picture Library; 124-125 AA/Mark Bauer; 127 AA/Caroline Jones; 128 AA/Nick Jenkins; 129 The Photolibrary Wales/Alamy; 131 AA/Mark Bauer; 132 AA; 133 AA/Roger Coulam; 134tl Private Collection/The Bridgeman Art Library; 134b AA/Roger Coulam; 135 AA/T Wyles; 136bl The British Library/Photolibrary; 136t Graeme Peacock/Alamy; 137 Nigel Reed QEDimages/Alamy; 138 Private Collection/Look and Learn/The Bridgeman Art Library; 139bl The Trustees of the British Museum; 139br Dae Sasitorn/www.lastrefuge.co.uk; 140-141 AA/Roger Coulam; 142 AA/Roger Coulam; 143bl Hulton Archive/Getty Images; 143tr Alan Sorrell/English Heritage. NMR/The Bridgeman Art Library; 144bl AA/Roger Coulam; 145 AA/Roger Coulam; 146 AA/Ken Paterson; 148tl Illustrated London News; 148b Private Collection/The Bridgeman Art Library; 149 AA/David Clapp; 150-151 AA/David Clapp; 152 Sabena Jane Blackbird/Alamy; 153 The Bridgeman Art Library/Getty; 154 Mary Evans Picture Library/Alamy; 155t AA/David Clapp; 155c AA/David Clapp; 156-157 AA/Linda Whitwam; 158 AA/David Clapp; 159bl Peter Brooker/Rex Features; 159tr David Hockney - Salts Mill, Saltaire, Yorkshire, 1997 oil on canvas. Photo Steve Oliver; 160 Mary Evans Picture Library; 161 AA/Wyn Voysey; 162-163 The National Trust Photolibrary/Alamy; 164 Moodboard/Robert Harding; 165 National Trust/Andrew Moss; 167 NTPL/Andrew Butler; 168 AA/Karl Blackwell; 169 AA/Karl Blackwell; 170 AA/Karl Blackwell; 171bl AA/Karl Blackwell; 171tr AA/Karl Blackwell; 172-173 AA/Karl Blackwell; 174 AA/Karl Blackwell; 175tc AA/Karl Blackwell; 175tr AA/Karl Blackwell; 176 AA/Karl Blackwell; 177 AA/Karl Blackwell; 178tl Private Collection/Archives Charmet/The Bridgeman Art Library; 178b Mary Evans Picture Library; 180-181 AA/Stephen Gibson; 182 Douglas Coltart, www.viridarium.co.uk; 184tl Mary Evans Picture Library; 184b Homer Sykes/Corbis; 185 Adrian Warren/www.lastrefuge.co.uk; 186-187 Iain Sarjeant/Photolibrary; 189 AA/Stephen Whitehorne; 190 Orkneypics/Alamy; 192 Chris Gomersall/Alamy; 193 National Trust for Scotland Photo Library/Alexander Bennett; 194-195 Colin Monteath/Photolibrary; 196bl Sharky/Alamy; 196br Nigel McCall/Alamy; 197 University of Aberdeen; 198 Adrian Warren/www.lastrefuge.co.uk; 199 Crown Copyright: RCAHMS. Licensor www.rcahms.gov.uk; 200 Chris Hill/Scenic Ireland; 201tl Colin Palmer Photography/Alamy; 201tr Chris Hill/Scenic Ireland; 202-203 Christian Handl/Photolibrary; 204 Chris Hill/Scenic Ireland; 205tl Photograph reproduced courtesy the Trustees of National Museums Northern Ireland; 205br Photograph reproduced courtesy the Trustees of National Museums Northern Ireland; 207 Sheila Halsall/Alamy; 208 AA/A Mockford & N Bonetti; 211 Andy Marshall/Alamy; 212-213 AA/Mark Hamblin; 217 AA/Hugh Palmer; Endpaper - Sandro Vannini/Corbis.

Every effort has been made to trace the copyright holders, and we apologise in advance for any accidental errors. We would be happy to apply any corrections in the following edition of this publication.